CHRISTIAN
IN THE
MARKET PLACE

CHRISTIAN IN THE MARKET PLACE

by **KARL RAHNER, S.J.**

translated by Cecily Hastings

SHEED & WARD · NEW YORK

© *Sheed and Ward Ltd.*, 1966

Originally published as Sendung und Gnade,
Tyrolia-Verlag, Innsbruck-Wein-Munchen, 1959

Published in England under the title Mission and Grace, Vol. III

Library of Congress Catalog Card Number 66-22022

Nihil obstat: Johannes M. T. Barton, S.T.D., L.S.S.
Imprimatur: Patritius Casey, Vic. Gen.
Westmonasterii, die 24a. Februarii 1966

Manufactured in the United States of America

Contents

CHRISTIAN
IN THE
MARKET PLACE

I

Paul, Apostle for Today

It is not my wish to give you, the members of the Paulus-Gesellschaft, anything really in the way of a theological lecture. Nor a talk on the organization and strategy of the lay apostolate in the modern age. I cannot talk here about the doctrine of St. Paul; yet it is on him that I want to keep my gaze focused. What I want is rather to draw on him for some ideas and suggestions and present them, quite unpretentiously, to you.

I can, for a start, propose two theses:

1. Every Christian is an apostle by the very nature of his Christianity, at all times and in all places. To be a Christian and to be an apostle are fundamentally identical.

2. Any Christian can be an apostle on the basis of any Christian situation. All that is essential is that he should have a right understanding of his own actual Christian situation. This means apostolate as the identification of our Christian existence with our present situation, whatever that may be.

Every Christian an Apostle

If we talk about the apostolate, what matters most is to be clear about it: we are not talking about a sideline, or about "eager-beaverdom," or any other kind of activity serving

3

egotistical aims and interests. Every Christian is an apostle, which means that he is an apostle just so far as he is a Christian.

There are many important and useful tasks, involving a great deal of activity, undertaken by priests and laymen in the name of the apostolate: auxiliary parish work, for instance. But you, as friends of the Paulus-Gesellschaft, are perfectly right to say: "I am not involved in that. My apostolate is one that arises from the possibilities within my own situation in my profession, in my marriage, in my family, in society." Not every form of activity, though seeming outwardly very attractive, qualifies as "apostolate." This is said simply as a warning against large, pious-sounding talk which does not come honestly and sincerely from the heart, its real motives being very personal and egotistic.

Nor, of course, does any reference to apostolate here mean the official apostolate of the hierarchy, the pastoral office of priest and bishop. I need not waste any space on this point.

It is not such a very easy matter, taking St. Paul for our starting-point, to arrive at the thesis that every Christian is an apostle. For there does not seem to be much reference to the apostolate in St. Paul. Not even to the apostolate of the hierarchy. Not, at least, as regards any special doctrines and principles. Paul himself is conscious of his own mission: he preaches the gospel, he knows that he is in the service of his Christ, to whom he totally belongs. But as for doctrine and directives about the methods and principles of Christian missionary work in the various churches . . . ? Do we find, anywhere in St. Paul's letters, exhortations like "You have got to convert the rest of men! Bring Jews and pagans along with you when you meet for worship. Persuade them to come to

sermons with you." For Paul it is all much simpler, more
natural, more straightforward.

But Christianity does make progress. And Paul can testify
that the fame of his communities has gone abroad beyond the
limits of their own area. So each Christian must have been
bearing witness, have been acting like an apostle, as a Christian chosen by grace, called and sanctified by God.

What does this simple fact mean to us Christians today?
Obviously, the Christians of that time did not meet with uniform success. On the contrary, the successes of Christianity
were at that time extremely modest. So many Jews won over
at once as Christians! Followed, of course, by large numbers
of relapses. Certainly, many Jews and pagans came to hear
Christian preaching and see Christian worship. They would
look and listen for a while, find it all quite interesting, and
then go off again and subside irretrievably into disbelief and
paganism. Their former lack of interest and religious indifference caught up with them again. It was no different then
from now.

But the first Christians did not lose courage over all this.
With a sense of being on the offensive, they went on testifying
to their Christianity. To them, it seemed something encour-
aging and wonderful to find so much as a person here and
there in the world who proved to be open to the light of
Christ.

We Christians today have a sense of being on the defensive. But only because we have got the idea that Christianity
ought, today, to be the most completely obvious thing in the
world. We think that the normal, traditionally established
activity of the Church should automatically make anyone
a Christian if he once comes within reach of it. So, since the

Church's apostolate ought to be so vastly and wonderfully effective, it strikes us as a scandal that everybody does not immediately become Christians when barely challenged to do so.

When it seems as though more Christians are falling away than being brought in, we give way to pessimism, as though our whole apostolate were doomed to collapse. Yet there is no discernible reason why, despite the magnificence of traditional, hierarchical Christianity, we should not be able to take up the same position as St. Paul: that Christianity is a sheer miracle of grace, the precise opposite of anything obvious and natural. In this way we Christians of today could have once more the sense of being on the offensive, just like the Christians of St. Paul's time: that the paganism in the world is the obvious thing, and Christianity in this world is the great miracle, God's free grace.

Three Difficulties

There are three difficulties confronting the thesis that every Christian is an apostle precisely because he is a Christian.

We today have got to acknowledge that we cannot simply and without more ado adopt St. Paul's standpoint. Paul is, of course, an absolute norm for a believing Christian. But as Christians of the twentieth century, living in an age of traditional, officially hierarchical Christianity, we have reflected on and arrived at certain insights which Paul did not have. These insights and perceptions represent, on the one hand, an undoubted progress. But they are on the other hand a strong limitation on the apostolic impulse in us.

1. As Christians of this century in the Church we can no

longer think so pessimistically of the salvation of non-Christians as Paul could within the religious outlook of his age and as Christians could still do as late as the seventeenth century. For Paul, those who did not receive baptism were lost. True, he did not propound any dogma about this. But in practice this was, for him, something obvious. This was the perspective within which he did his missionary work. Right on to the late Middle Ages and beyond, Christians to a large extent derived their missionary impulse from this view.

We, as Christians of the twentieth century, can no longer conform to this perspective and practice. Indeed, we must not. A missionary today can no longer hold the conviction that, say, Francis Xavier still had: If I go to the Japanese and teach them and preach Christ to them, they will be saved and go to heaven. But if I stay in Europe, they will be lost, as their forefathers were lost, because they never heard of Christ and died without baptism. A person penetrated by a conviction of this sort will, of course, necessarily feel himself driven by an extremely strong missionary impulse. He will employ every possible means of word and prayer and sacrifice to convert the unbeliever.

Our religious sense as Christians today is different. We find it difficult to suppose that people who have never heard of Christ are eternally damned. We cannot share this outlook from a dogmatic point of view, either. Today, we know that there is an invisible Christianity which does indeed possess the justification of sanctifying grace from God. A man belonging to this invisible Christianity may deny his Christianity or maintain that he does not know whether he is a

Christian or not—that he is not even sure whether Christ is the Son of God. Yet God may have chosen him in grace.

If the Holy Father were giving an audience to a person of another belief, he would not start by saying, "My son, be converted! Otherwise you will be lost. Not a word on any other subject! We will leave all our other problems on one side." I feel sure that a pope of, say, the sixteenth century would still have spoken in this kind of way. No pope today is going to call in question the value of discussions on such things as social problems on the ground that the first thing to do is to save these people's souls.

Thus something has penetrated into our religious sense, something that does not in the least need to involve lukewarmness or anything unchristian. But we have got to acknowledge that our missionary impulse has suffered by it; that it no longer has the intensity that it had in earlier ages of the Church's history.

2. It is part of the historical situation, it is a fact about our time, that we today are more consciously aware of the gulf between God and man. God in his greatness and splendor —man in his littleness and fragility. The distance between the inconceivable God, inexpressibly exalted above everything other than himself, impenetrably mysterious, and the existence that we have.

Whereas the Christian of earlier times saw the ascension of Christ within the framework of his natural picture of the world, involving no conflict with the data of physics as he knew them, today this is very much otherwise. There is no ground for stating that the old image was in some way more Christian or more natural than that of today. But God and man were, in imagination, closer to each other. Because of this, a man of that time was able to have a more naive feeling about the absolute character of religion in the concrete, with all its regulations and practices, than we men of today can have. This is a fact.

Since we are Christians, which means being honest and sincere, we have got to acknowledge this difficulty with honesty and sincerity. If this wisdom about the faith, which the faith itself demands, gets right into my blood and my feelings and my whole sense of existence, then I am going to have a certain difficulty about any naive impulse towards the apostolate. Naturally, even for us of today religion has its quite definite truths and its particular practices which we regard as absolute. But because of the historical fact of which I have spoken, we have certain inhibitions restricting the naive élan with which we are prepared to preach these truths and practices.

You have only to take the example of your own religious life and to think of the model provided by your devout parents. Obviously, a Christian of today still knows about his duty to be at the holy sacrifice of the Mass every Sunday. But it must be admitted that it is harder for a person of today than for a Christian of two hundred years ago really to enter into this idea and make it real to himself. Not because a person of today is less interested in God. But because God seems so infinitely exalted to us men of today, so inconceivably great, that one is tempted to think that human beings can show him no greater honor than by keeping quiet about him. I am not maintaining that a feeling of this sort is bound to be always and in all respects Christian. It is possible for a certain arrogance to smuggle itself into an attitude of this kind. But the feeling is nevertheless there, and it involves a certain difficulty for any naive élan in us towards the apostolate.

Added to this, there is often the difficulty for the modern hearer in the way in which the faith is formulated. For the last few weeks, I have been preparing a woman student for reception into the Catholic Church. Throughout the instructions, the doubt kept occurring to me: Am I saying the truths of our faith to this girl in such a concrete and real way that this human being is going to be able to live in them and by them? That they are going to become an existential reality for her? Earlier, Christians felt and learned their faith quite simply and naively. Today this is harder for us. Why is there scarcely ever a sermon about the return of Christ? An ordinary lay Christian, living in his parish, never hears a word of it. Nor, probably, is he interested in it. How many preachers, apart from missioners, ever talk about hell? Hell and the return of Christ are, of course, part of the matter taught in any catechism. There is no dispute about either of these truths as belonging to our faith. But how hard it is to state such truths today as having such reality that the hearer has any possibility of taking hold of them even as thinkable representations of a concrete reality. How difficult it is altogether to confess our faith before the world in a really apostolic way, and not get held up in the outer fringes of Christianity. Yet we have got to lay the foundations for the acceptance of these truths in the world. We have got to state the things of our faith in such a way that the faith itself can follow.

But we can be of good cheer. There are plenty of people committing themselves to Christ today: encountering him, loving him, recognizing him as Lord and Savior, receiving his word from him in an existential response.

3. The third obstacle is ourselves. No decent, honest man, still less any truly believing Christian, is going to deny that we are all wretched sinners in need of the grace of God. There is no disputing this ultimate fact: we are not what we ought to be. We are a mass of faults and weaknesses. We are arrogant, conceited, egotistic. Nor is there any sense in laying this on so thick as, in practice, to take the sting out of it. As Christians, we have to face the fact that it is possible for us to be damned through our own fault. This possibility is part of Christianity. And there is the danger that we today may fall below our quota in responsibility for our fellow-men: that we may fail in our apostolate.

If there is an apostolate of grace, a real responsibility for one's brother's soul and his eternal salvation, then we cannot say, "All we owe our fellow-men is to be nice to them and to struggle for social progress" (which is, of course, a thing that can have a completely Christian meaning in the eyes of God and his judgment, not only in the eyes of Communists). We are responsible for our brother in terms of the real possibility that he may be damned, with ourselves to blame for it. We cannot fulfill this responsibility by doing nothing, taking things easy, or plunging into our day-to-day work and "never having time." We have got to acknowledge that at this point or that we are not doing what we should and could do. The crucial, final difficulty for our apostolate is our own unconverted hearts: we ourselves.

There is no simple historical solution to this difficulty, enabling us to lay the blame on others, who do, no doubt, have their faults as well. My brother's soul may be required at my hand. Just at what point it becomes my responsibility is difficult to say in any individual case. But we have got to reckon with the real possibility of being guilty in this way.

If man is faced with an eternal destiny, and one which he has to create for himself, freely, no matter what darkness he may be in; and if we have a personal obligation to help our fellow-men out of this darkness: then we are always liable to be asked the question "Where is your brother?" And then the question may be whether we shall perhaps lose our own souls because we have not concerned ourselves with our brother's soul.

It is perfectly true that we cannot go on to deduce, from this responsibility of mine, that it is my duty to be a member of the Christian Democrat Party, or attend the Katholikentag at Berlin, or wear a badge or give lectures or lead a discussion group. How this responsibility for my brother's soul translates itself into concrete terms in my life and is worked out there is another question altogether. But as to whether the apostolate is part of our being Christians, seeing that the love of our fellow-men is one of the demands, indeed the fundamental demand of Christianity, as to whether it is a life-and-death constituent of our own existence as Christians, there can be no doubt at all. And it is here that we ourselves are the ultimate and crucial difficulty.

Meeting Each of the Three Difficulties

The first difficulty affecting our missionary impulse is that I have to accept the fact that my brother does have a possibility of salvation without me.

But this cannot, in the last analysis, determine my own existential attitude. I assent theologically to the truth and the possibility that men are saved without belonging visibly to the Church or even to historical Christianity, but I cannot draw from it the conclusion that therefore I do not need to engage in any apostolic activity.

There are many truths which, precisely because they are true, call for great caution, having regard to their existential implications, if they are to be translated into imperative terms. The ultimate decision of the destiny of any man lies within the concrete life of this world. What is crucial for me is what is done within this concrete life—not what happens beyond the limits of this life. Now I know, from the teaching of my faith, that God gives every man as much grace as he needs to save himself. God wills that all men should be saved, says St. Paul. But it may be God's will that I should intervene in favor of this particular man. If I fail, no doubt God will give him grace even without me. God writes straight with crooked lines. The ultimate depth of grace is revealed in this, that God lets good come out of evil. But woe to that man who thinks that this means he can usurp God's position: that he can do evil that good may come. Woe to that man who thinks that he can outwit God. But this is what we should be trying to do if we made the possibility of salvation outside God's normal means of salvation into a basis for the conclusion that we have no apostolic task, or no urgent one: that God has no need of us human beings. This sense of being responsible for my brother, not only for his earthly needs but precisely for his eternal salvation, may be nothing short of decisive for my own eternal salvation.

This is not sublime egoism. The realization that unless one loves selflessly one is risking one's own salvation does not imply some higher form of egoism. It is the scale by which I can measure how absolutely necessary is concern for my brother's salvation. The possibility that he has of working out his salvation without me means that he owes me nothing. But I can find myself only if I find my brother.

The whole of life has got to be a forward movement towards loving my brother. I must love my brother, and in that love forget myself. If I do that, I am an apostle. If I do not do it, I am ultimately lost. The realization that it is possible for the other person to work out his salvation without me need not have any damping effect on my apostolate. On the contrary, its effect may well be positive: impressing on me the fact that, because he is placed already within the possibility of salvation, he is accessible to what I have to say to him.

St. Francis Xavier tried to convert people concerning whom he thought that they were simply and totally in the power of the devil. We Christians of today have to regard even apparent unbelievers as "anonymous" Christians. Surely our apostolate must in fact come more easily to us. But what we need to be able to do is to declare our Christianity in such a way that the other person senses that what he is being urged to become is really what in the depths of his heart he perhaps already is.

Thus the first of these difficulties need not be any hindrance to our apostolate. On the contrary, it might well release the forces of our apostolic impulse, make it freer and less inhibited. But only on condition that we gradually learn to overcome the second difficulty.

This second difficulty was that it is a fact of our times that it is more difficult for us than for the people of an earlier time to have a naive sense of religion in the concrete as an absolute.

In this connection, we have to remember that many people

are going to remain pagans. And many people are going to be
reached only by Christianity in small doses. What God asks
of us is that the grace with which, perhaps without us and
by ways that remain impenetrable to us, he saves very many
men should also be given explicitly official, ecclesiastical testimony: that this, which lives in the depths of very many
hearts, the grace by which Christ has achieved salvation in
his love and his obedience, should also become something
manifest. As to what reception is given to the word which
expresses this inner reality, this is a secondary question. But
it is God's will in any case that grace in its historical visibility,
the visible deed and visible sacrifice of Christ, should live on
in our witness to it. God does not will that the salvation of
all men should be in the depth of their consciences. He wills
that it should be in Jesus Christ, who is made flesh. To be
not only an anonymous Christian, but to know what one is
—this is grace.

It is our apostolate to witness to Christianity in its visibility.
For it is thus that Christ willed to reveal his grace—in visible
witness. Clearly, if men who have been made by grace into
anonymous Christians are to be moved, beyond this, to bear
visible testimony to this Christianity in their lives, our second
difficulty is going to have to be decisively overcome.

We in the Paulus-Gesellschaft need to think very seriously
about how we are to make ourselves, in this sense, more and
more Christian, so that our Christianity does not continue to
be something we accept as a sort of "package deal." It has got
to be "assimilated" by us, transformed, so to speak, into our
own flesh and blood, so that we can live it convincingly in the
sight of others and speak of it to them. Our apostolate to ourselves must always remain our most urgent task. And fraternal

correction must also be our task, so that we tell the theologians, when what they say is completely unintelligible. We have got to try, as Christians, to be illuminating. Then this will make our apostolate to other people fruitful, too.

The third difficulty affecting our missionary élan is we ourselves, the most important hindrance to our apostolate.

This hindrance is one that can only be overcome by ourselves. Hard as this truth is for us, we have got to acknowledge it, and strive to become better Christians and thus better apostles.

Every Situation an Apostolate

Every Christian, being by his very Christianity an apostle, can fulfill this apostleship in every situation: profession, marriage, family, society. I think that we often make the apostolate impossible for ourselves by not beginning it honestly in the very place where we find ourselves. In the case of the lay apostle in particular, who, while he does bear witness to official, hierarchical Christianity, does not himself, essentially, have an official commission, this witness must, in a radical way, be borne above all in the private sphere. Every Christian has got to give his own testimony, by bearing essential witness to Christianity through his existence as a Christian. This takes place more directly in a lay Christian than in an officially appointed bearer of the message, because the latter is bound to be talking "above himself" in what he says. The whole witness of the lay Christian is given through himself and his life in his profession, marriage, family, society. Obviously, an apostolate of this sort has got to begin at the point where this particular concrete person actually finds himself. He cannot jump out of himself and his concrete Christian situation. He does not need to talk insincerely and bombastically about things with which he himself is as yet by no means *au fait*. Every concrete situation in which a person finds himself has to be seen as a positive opportunity for his own Christian life and his witness to it.

Christianity is not a thing which can be either present or absent. While it is God's free gift, it is, by the very fact that it exists, always present. The only question is, always, whether what is here present is being rightly handled. Every personal situation that a person can be in, whether he be well or ill, highly talented or not, feeling remote from God or full of a sense of freedom and devotion, can be an occasion of positive Christianity. None of this is negative: it has all got to be positively evaluated and used to the full. It is thus that I perceive the immeasurable splendor of God. There is no situation which cannot represent an opportunity for our Christianity. I think that if we as Christians act from our situation, in all freedom, we shall find it easier to bear witness.

I am not talking about some sort of device which, if cunningly applied, will round up untold numbers for the fold of Christ. Our apostolate is always necessarily going to issue in non-observability and apparent lack of success. But at the same time we do not need to make unnecessary difficulties for ourselves. We must practice our apostolate from the point at which we have our own place in the world. This was so with St. Paul. By not channeling the Gentiles through Judaism, by not radically combating the Gentile world, Paul asserted in general terms the principle that every human being is to become a Christian from the point at which he himself is placed. One's own concrete spiritual situation is, when rightly understood in its ultimate intention, a possibility granted to one of becoming a Christian and being an apostle.

We must bear responsibility for the salvation of our brothers and sisters. But we can be confident in the conviction that we are not under an obligation to perform actions of a kind remote from our concrete situation. We are Christians and, by that fact, apostles—in every situation and through every situation in which God has placed us. We should not obscure this task, which is truly our own, by proposing to ourselves some other which is foreign to us, rightly excusing ourselves from it, as not having been given to us, and then making this an occasion for withdrawing equally from the task that has indeed been entrusted to us.

The Paulus-Gesellschaft may well help us, in brotherly association with each other, to carry out our apostolate in the world. This is something that makes sense. And precisely because an association of this sort does make sense, there does not need to be only one of it: just as a particular religious Order makes sense, and hence there can well be several such. We do not need to look on other societies as competitors. But nor do we need to feel unsure of ourselves because of other societies. We are not an organization for a particular status or interests. We are an association whose members help each other in the task of a living apostolate on the basis of personal friendship or acquaintance. This is the justification for our existence. But we must certainly realize clearly that having this meaning, of a direct encounter between people who are convinced that they are called to the apostolate by the grace of God as Christians, the Paulus-Gesellschaft, in its spirit and its aims, is always going to be an affair of few rather than many people.

2

Railway Missions

The Bavarian union of Catholic societies for the protection
of young girls is today celebrating its foundation, sixty years
ago. It is invoking its past, as a pledge of blessing upon the
future; it is turning back in thought to its origins, the better
to find a way through its present tasks; it is giving thanks
to the Giver of all good gifts and begging for his blessing
upon the mission that lies before it. What is there to be said
in such an hour of celebration? What can be said by one who
cannot boast that he has shared the burden and heat of the
day, one who is required to live exiled and excluded from the
direct service of charity and human beings in a world of
theory, which, even when concerned with God and eternal
life, is always a little drab? It is obvious that it cannot be my
task in these few words to say anything very "practical," very
relevant and applicable to the daily labors and anxieties, the
new methods and tasks, which are part of the burden, and
the grace, of this association. Further, the working conference which is going to follow on from this will provide the
opportunity for these things. Nor would it be possible for
me, on such an occasion, to recount the history of these sixty
years. For of this, too, almost all of you know more than I do;
nor could any adequate account be given of it in one short
hour. But there is one thing that we can do, one thing that

even a theologian can be confident in doing: on this day when we are commemorating historical beginnings, to say something of the origins of this work that lie within the thing itself; not its origins in time, but in the eternal nature of things and in God; those origins which do not stretch back into the past but are so much an eternal present that it is really only possible to preserve the future as a living future if one takes possession more and more of these origins and enters more and more deeply into them.

The thing that is to be said can be summed up in one sentence: a new historical situation now confronts the old task —old and ever new—and out of the fusion of task and situation will emerge the new service to which this association, whose jubilee we are celebrating, is committed and dedicated. So we have to talk about

1. The new historical situation, which calls for a new service to human beings;

2. The task, ever the same, which devolves upon the Church and the Christian;

3. The new service, in which the old task in the new situation will take concrete form.

The New Historical Situation

Man is spirit, achieving consciousness, thinking about himself; and he is history, involved in perpetual change. And because he is both, he can fulfill his nature only by reflecting on the historical situation in which he is placed and which is propelling him forward towards God's eternity, so that, in thus reflecting on himself as historically conditioned, he actuates his spiritual being, and thus at the same time propels his own history towards its destination. Much has been said, much more than can be summarized, about the special character of the age in which we are living, the particular age in which we, being caught in it as in our destiny, have to work out our own salvation or damnation in the indissoluble unity of historical necessity and personal freedom. Our times have been described as the end of the modern age; as the atomic age; as the age of unification in one human history of all who dwell on the one planet; as the age of organized atheism; of worldwide industrialism; of the collective, of man in the mass, of the decline of individualism and interest in subjective personality; as the age of existential anguish, disillusion, and loss of belief in progress; the age of the denaturing of nature, the eclipse of the numinous in the world, the absence of God; of the substitution of the planned product for the natural growth, of addiction and anxiety, of the replacement of the given by the manufactured, of loss of the center; an age in which, for the first time, the release of the mind from its bondage to nature is really being accomplished.

Many such descriptions, and others besides, are given, whether as hymns in praise of the new age or as denunciations of the devil in the sheep's clothing of a new age. It is not our business here to criticize these various attempts at description: some of them profound, some premature, some comprehensive, some one-sided, some optimistic, some pessimistic, some within the terms of this world, some eschatological. Still less can we venture to make any better or more comprehensive suggestion of our own. But there is surely one thing that they have got right: they surely prove that this sense of standing on the threshold of a new historical epoch is not merely an effect of that exaggerated self-esteem common to every generation, which always thinks itself the beginning of a new age. We are indeed in the midst of a transition (though the transition itself constitutes a long period) from one epoch to another, with a greater difference between them than what necessarily separates one century from another in a world in which no state of affairs is permanent. It is probable that we are liable only to underestimate this change, not to overestimate it; developments have been set in motion whose end and scale are altogether beyond our sight and reckoning. A world whose history has once more become one—as one might say theologically, for the first time since the Tower of Babel—a world in which the destiny of every man is dependent on that of every other, a world in which man reaches into the innermost structure of material things created by God and no longer merely makes use of them in the form in which they themselves, i.e. as coming from God, offer themselves to him, a world in which man no longer enjoys the fruits of the earth but creates them himself—such a world really is, to an unimaginable degree, new and different, so new that it is all too difficult for many people to see that the inmost essential reality of the world as God's creation has not, after all, changed, that man cannot, after all, make everything, and that the ultimate thing still eludes his wilful grasp: his own nature in its inescapable relationship to God.

We really do live in a new situation, in comparison with which the whole history of humanity and of Christianity so far, despite all its vicissitudes and changes, really does shrink into a single period. The transition from one period to another lasts for a long time, longer than an individual man's life; we are inescapably creatures of yesterday and today and tomorrow. If anyone, impatiently revolutionary, seeks to cast off the historical necessity of living in this state of transition, he will merely fail in what has been appointed for him in history; he will be serving, not the future, but destruction; he will not be laying hold on the wealth to come but losing that heritage from his forefathers which he was meant to take with him into the future as something too precious to be lost. But we are indeed in transition. And anyone who looks squarely at this situation with confidence in God and accepts it, not taking refuge in the past or despairing of the future, is making a contribution, within God's grace, to the carrying forward of God's kingdom into the future, regardless of whether that future proves to be the end of all the ages or a new period in the age before the end.

As I have said already, it cannot be my task here and now to describe this future which, being the goal, determines the special character of the road we are travelling in the present. I will only try to clarify one feature of this situation we are in, which seems important for our further deliberations. We might perhaps say: Man used to be entrusted to nature, given into her protection, but today, and more emphatically still tomorrow, it is he himself who will have to protect himself, his essential being and his eternal destiny, for to a great extent he will no longer be protected by nature. Of course, a description of this sort is always a matter of degree, not of a radical either-or. Man will always remain a natural being, he will never entirely bypass what comes to him from the Creator as given, he will always have a starting-point, an origin, which is imposed upon him and not subject to his own choice, limiting the possibilities for his discovery and determination of himself. And always, even in the most distant past, man was a being with freedom, freedom to dispose of himself and shape himself, a being who does not merely do things but enacts himself.

Nevertheless, there is this difference between yesterday and tomorrow. The God of history is entrusting man to an increasing degree to himself, whereas he used to protect him much more from himself by confining him within the necessity of nature. Whether in accordance with or against God's will (and how hard it is to distinguish these two possibilities from each other), man is wresting dominion more and more to himself. This is something that happens in the history of mankind in general: the child is protected against his environment and especially against himself by others, his parents, his kindred; the adult is given over to his own protection, his own responsibility. Man used to be protected by what is imposed and inescapable, which is nature. He could not be everywhere, he had to be sedentary, whether he liked it or not; the abiding sameness of his environment forced him, without his observing it, to a traditional way of life. He had no weapons that would enable him to kill large numbers of people before being killed himself; he could not escape from the unity and closed structure of family and kindred without being swiftly punished by the loss of his biological existence; the number of his progeny was not something over which, in the concrete, he was in a position to exercise control; nationalism and internationalism were no problem in periods in which peoples were isolated from each other by empty areas; intellectual events had plenty of time to develop and ripen slowly, because, without printing, radio and similar things, it was not possible artificially to accelerate such developments and work them to death; man could not over-stimulate himself with addictions and sensations; he could not get away from himself, he could not achieve the fearful discontinuity of modern life, because to a large extent he simply did not have the wherewithal, and because even small attempts to do so would be promptly disciplined on the spot by nature, with punishments going as far as death. In short, man was protected against himself by nature, by what was other than himself, by what was imposed on him. Much that was essentially right in his life, much of his morality, was the effect, not of his freedom responsibly exercised, but of the salutary compulsion practiced by Mother Nature on her still infantile offspring, man, allowing him only relatively narrow scope for acts of freedom.

Today it is different. Man is beginning to carry out the task, laid on him in paradise, of subduing the earth, on a hitherto unimaginable scale. There is nowhere where he cannot go. He can control his own breeding processes, he can make artificial materials that are better than those provided by nature; he can plan himself; he is even thinking of leaving behind this earth which God created as man's home; he bounces radar signals off the moon, which God set in the sky to be his light by night, and which men of an earlier age reverently contemplated as an unattainable heavenly image of a wholly other world, not subject to terrestrial change; he no longer knows of any starry heaven above him to fill him with the same awe as the moral law within his heart; he has no convictions which could not be confuted, not by arguments and in the light of higher truth, but by the right injection. He has been largely successful in protecting himself against nature, which he sees as cruel and heartless towards man; he has reared ramparts against her, against her climate and her bacteria, her animals and her powers of death. And behold, in protecting himself against nature he has lost the protection which she afforded him against himself, and man is delivered defenseless into his own hands, to all the errant possibilities of his freedom, to his own hybris, to his everlasting temptation to be as God, i.e. to be someone bound by no reality outside himself, no law higher than himself. Now no one can protect him from himself except himself as he is when he is more than himself, that is, when God in his grace is with him.

The new situation is a situation of man's defenselessness against himself, and he in his sinfulness is crueller to himself than the whole of nature, against which he can now protect himself. Man, escaped from nature—protective, nurturing, limiting, formative nature—is handed over to himself, to his destructive intemperance and lack of intellectual bounds. During the time that God, the Creator of man, was saving him from himself by means of nature, during the time that nature and her imperious law was acting as God's pedagogue, directing man to God and his own healthy estate, man has been growing up. And God himself, his dealings with man now being direct, can protect man from himself. What the new situation means is that man, removed from the protection of nature, must now seek from God the protection against himself that he needs for the fulfillment of his being. And first we must go on to say what it is that must be protected, and in what directions, in this new situation, in which man must himself play the role of his own guardian angel.

The Unchanging Task Devolving upon the Church and the Christian

This unchanging task is concerned with man: with man as he really is, as, in derivation from God, he is really meant

to be, hence as man and as Christian. For however much nature and grace can and must be theoretically distinguished as
two orders, yet in the operation of real life these two orders
depend on each other in the one man, and neither can be
saved and preserved without the other. Hence we can simply
say that the unchanging task is man, the one being. Because
of his eternal essential being, because he carries that being on
through all the changes of history, the task always remains
the same as of old. Because this one eternal essential being
always has to be preserved and fulfilled afresh in ever chang-
ing historical situations, it is a task that is always new, and
it is only in this perpetually new task that man experiences
the whole immeasurable breadth and fullness of his own
being. Hence, again, his history, for all that it has a permanent
ground of essential being, is not a monotonous repetition of
sameness but a single, unique drama, in which what man is
really and in truth meant to be is made concretely manifest
and explicit. But even though it is only out of the new situation that we come to learn, in the concrete, what man is, yet
this history in which man acts and achieves realization of himself issues from an initial knowledge of his abiding essence,
at which he arrives by the light of his natural reason and
through the word of revelation. Hence we can say what this
ancient and permanent task is, however much of a surprise
it always is to us, as we look around us in the light of the
knowledge we have from God, to see the new ways in which
the old task has to be carried out.

It is concerned with man. Thus it is concerned with the
preservation of what is human; with man, a single being, who
is bodily spirit and spiritual body; with the defense of the
spirit and its scope for freedom; with the dignity of the per-

son, who is not to be made a means to other ends; with man in the pattern and structure of his own nature, with its subordinate and superior levels, its single element of necessity and its multitude of contingent and provisional elements; with man, who is more than an atom in a human society; man, who has an eternal destiny; man, who is only as he should be when he possesses reverence, loyalty and truthfulness, when he has learned to love and to serve; man who is required to abide and endure himself, and not to escape, abdicating his spiritual nature, either into obsessive pleasures or work or any other occupation. It is concerned with man, who is created as man and woman, and who can find his destiny only as one or the other; the different ages of whose life are not to be regarded as all on a dead level, but who is able to embark upon something at each of these levels; man who has his place in society to fill, while remaining something more in it, and becoming something more through it, than a mere function of a collective regarded as an end in itself. It is concerned with man, who is open to God, the nameless, unfathomable, unutterable; and hence with man the undefinable, man the mystery, man who belongs to eternity and infinity, who cannot stop short anywhere in this world, who cannot be defined by anything terrestrial and demonstrable, who in the immeasurable scope of his spirit and his love sees everything as relative except that one unutterable One whom we call God: who can only be God, in himself and in regard to us, if he is not identified with anything that can be grasped in this world or with the sum of what can thus be grasped. In short, it is concerned with man as open towards God.

It is concerned with the Christian. For if man is open towards the real and living God, then he is a Christian, whether he knows it or not. For God has called man in Jesus Christ, called him into his own life, graced him with a share in his own nature, his own glory and his own life. It is not his will to impart this glory only in a process taking place within the ultimate depths of man's being and conscience in an imperceptible way; he wills that this saving event of the gracious justification of man with the divine life of the Trinity should become a tangible event in Jesus Christ, the Father's Word made flesh; in his visible Church; in the tangible event of the sacraments; in the audible word of the message of salvation; in the holy lives and actions of those who have received grace; in the slowly accomplished transfiguration of the whole cosmos. It is concerned, then, with man who, in this concrete way, in the whole breadth and fullness of his personal and social life, accepts this God of grace, believes his message, hopes in his promise, responds to his love with a return of grace-given love; who develops faith, hope and love and brings them to fulfillment in the living of a truly human life: a life that is pure, loving, humble, hopeful, confident, patient, enduring; until time becomes eternity and history one single fulfillment in the glory of God, which the Son receives from eternity from the Father and possesses in the love of the Holy Spirit.

This is the man with whom it is concerned: the Christian, the man of eternity, the son of God, heir to the promise, temple of the Spirit, living in death, victor in all the defeats of time. It is always this one same whole man and Christian in all the partial operations of life, whether small or great, whether everyday matters or the high points of life; always and everywhere, even where he seems only to be engaged in the pursuit of earthly survival, he has to be a man and a

Christian, and only if and in so far as he is this can the individual operations and dimensions of his life remain healthy. For when man's life has no outlet into the infinity of God, the energy of his spirit, whose only adequate object is the infinite God, converts itself into a self-destructive force, equally destructive whether it emerges as power-hungry hybris, or as nausea at the cramped dreariness of endless existence, or as a senseless, meandering hunger for pleasure to dull the tedium of life.

That is the task, ever old and ever new: man himself, the Christian, in his eternal destiny, which is always one and the same: the living, eternal God, who has given himself to us in Jesus Christ our Lord, in his Spirit, and his one Church.

The New Service

But what has all this to do with what we have come together to celebrate? It has everything to do with it. For it is only if we take the new situation and the old task of which we have been speaking, and bring them together, so that the two combine and become one, that we shall be able to grasp the ultimate essence of this association whose jubilee we are keeping.

In the first place:

The task which this association sets itself is that one task, in its completeness, of which we have been speaking. Of course it is not alone in setting itself this task. This is the task of Jesus Christ himself, the task of the Church, of the hierarchy in its pastoral office and of every individual and association working for the salvation of souls. It is not alone in setting itself this task; nor, obviously, could it handle it alone. But this is what it sets itself, this and nothing else. This whole integral task. A society like this for the protection of young girls may give some young thing shelter for one night so that she need not be left to wander about the streets waiting for the morning and the next train to take her on her journey; what it sees in her is a human being, a Christian, eternal salvation, the whole person who belongs to God. This association is not a mere philanthropic society limiting itself to, and ultimately stifling itself in, what lies within this world. It is not a sort of third-party insurance taken out by the "haves" against the threat of social crises, not an organization for taking token payments from the rich for the poor so as to allow the donors to sleep undisturbed by uncomfortable feelings about the poor and socially depressed classes. What this association sees is the whole Christian human being, the child of God, the heir to eternal life, redeemed by the same blood of Christ as gives us all hope for our salvation. It sees a sister in Christ, someone whom one stands beside; not a person of a lower social order to whom one stoops in benevolent boredom.

The love thus extended is no less solid and substantial than it would be if all one really cared about, at bottom, were money and earthly welfare; if the help provided were merely an offer of compensation between social classes engaged, basically, in a war with each other; if one were acting only, in a nebulous way, in virtue of some very abstract human dignity, with no knowledge of what it really rests on or what is its ultimate guarantee. The ultimate basis of *caritas* is religious; it has this basis as a matter of practical fact and has, as a matter of history, grown up upon this basis and on nothing else; losing it would mean in the long run its death and degeneration into bureaucratic welfare. This does not make this *caritas* something with a distorted goal; what it seeks is simply man, every man, him and nothing else—but *him*, the beloved of God, the man with an eternal destiny. It is a love which cannot allow itself to be forbidden to see infinitely more in man than a mere man, a love which looks at man with the eyes of the wisdom of God and the love of the Holy Spirit, a love which co-operates in the creative graciousness of God. Hence this association can never be detached from its religious origins and its Christian roots; it cannot do other than desire to co-operate in the salvation of the whole single being, man, in God; it can never allow itself to be confined to merely earthly social welfare. The pattern for its service and its protection, what it cares for and what it protects, is man in his immortality: the ancient and all-embracing task of man and Christian. Hence, while this association may, by self-limitation, and in combination with the thousands of other and larger ones co-operating in the salvation of man, do only a fragment of the work by which this task is carried out, it can only remain alive if it is clearly and ever newly aware that it exists in the service of this one task, the whole man and the complete Christian.

But this all-embracing task, old and ever new, has entered on a new stage because of the new situation that I have been describing. But it is the very characteristic of this association for the protection of young girls to have recognized a new service in the old task. This service is of a new kind because the serving of this task, old and ever young, now calls for the taking over of that protection which in all earlier ages of humanity was provided by the maternal control, guidance and constraint of nature, at a time when her iron rule could not be overcome. We have been saying that, in comparison with earlier times, man is today, to a hitherto unimaginable degree, entrusted to himself, handed over to himself and to the potentially destructive powers of his own being. Today, man has to protect himself from himself, because nature, conquered and herself delivered over to man, no longer does it. The association for protecting young girls is one such alliance, for the protection of man by man, because he is no longer protected by the stringent ordinances of his own natural being.

This is not all a highbrow elaboration aimed at giving a simple matter of genuine Christian love some sort of interest-value within problematical historical theology. Quite the reverse. The great founder-figures of this association in Bavaria: Father Cyprian the Capuchin, Luise Fogt, Christiane von Preysing, Marie von Hohenhausen and, later, Ellen Ammann were not (it is to be hoped) much given to theorizing, but simply went to work according to the sure instinct of their unselfish, alert, responsible, active love. But what they did was, objectively, this new service of protecting defenseless man. It is not a matter of chance that the work began with missions on railway stations. A station is a symbol of the new age we have in mind, a symbol of freedom of movement, homelessness, unattachment; one of the symbols of technology; in short, a symbol of the new age in which man is becoming the master of nature, escaping from her power but also from her protection, and is in danger because there is nowhere where he cannot go. This association came into existence because the care of souls based on a particular place, rooted in the soil where people were naturally at home, was ceasing to be adequate; it accompanied man as he set out into the danger of losing himself.

Of course the exorcism of defenseless man from himself

and from the demons of his own being required many more means than those at the disposal of this association. At about that same time (in terms of world history) other new pastoral forces did in fact appear: professional associations, Christian parties, specialized pastoral work for social groups, etc. But its point of departure—the dangers threatening the traveller —its supranational, almost worldwide organization, and also its earlier date of foundation all show that this association really was a foundation of the Spirit of God in the Church, in which, with the unreflecting, naive, almost blind clear-sightedness of love, certain people perceived a new age, a new situation, and so a new way of serving the old task, and, for their part, put it into practice. Before, the church spire had been the center and symbol of human and Christian exist-ence, built in the midst of a stable home, where the ancestral house and the ties of kindred surrounded a man protectively all his life long; so that to go "into the wide world" meant the same as to go into exile and misery: the man in distress was simply the homeless man.[1] Today it is the railway sta-tion, amongst other things, that has become the symbol of our new home; and if a man is not to be wretched, he must travel and go abroad, restlessly and endlessly. Well, then— said this association—if the station is the sign of the times, then the station will have to become a church; the Church will have to be there, with yellow stripes to know her by, at the place where this stream of homeless human beings flows past, lifting up the sign of her faith in the eternal dignity of man and her love for all who have been redeemed by the blood of Christ. And so the association itself became a kind of symbol showing that the Church saw the new situation and accepted this new service of the old task: the protection of man, become defenseless in the new age, so that he should remain and become what he has to be: a man and a Christian.

When we now look at what came into existence sixty years ago as a new way of serving human beings, we can perhaps, along with all that was then seen and tackled with the genius of true love, add in one line of the picture which was then, perhaps, not so clearly seen. It may be that at that time this service was seen as a service of humble love on the part of the secure towards those in danger, rendered by those who still had their roots to those who were in the dangers of transit. We now know that we are all people who must, to a great extent, do without the protection of the rooted and organic, of what is imposed and handed down and can be taken for granted as natural; that we have become vulnerable transients ourselves. There is a greater and closer community of destiny between protectors and protected; the result should be something still more brotherly and sisterly, still further removed from all danger of that arrogant condescension which has never been anything other than a caricature of true Christian love. But this last feature, added to the new service by sixty years of world wars, revolutions, uprootings of populations and general upheavals, has done no more than confirm and deepen the basic conception of this association; it has simply made its task to an even greater extent a duty in which all are involved, for all are in danger, all stand in need of that protection which nature no longer provides, and hence all must accept a new responsibility for their brothers and sisters. Today, when everyone is in need of human protection if he and his environment are to stay healthy, no one can ever again ask Cain's question, "Am I my brother's keeper?" More than ever, our neighbor's soul is required at our hands. More than ever must man be the protector of man and Christian of Christian. More than ever must the human community, in all its structures, associations and organizations, bring to realization something of that spirit and responsibility which, sixty years ago, called into existence the association whose jubilee we are keeping today. This association cannot be alone in sustaining this new service in the old task in the new situation. Emphatically not. But we cannot grasp its significance and greatness unless we see in it, not just one more organization for one more useful charitable purpose, but one, though only one, concrete form of a service whose significance for the Church of our age and the future is absolute; a service which did not and could not exist in earlier times but is today among the Church's fundamental tasks.

Let us try to make this new service of humanity a little clearer still:

When we say that what this service means today is that man, in his apostolic care for the salvation of the man and the Christian in his neighbor, through responsible action, example, teaching, life, and help in all fields of Christian existence, now provides that protection which used to be provided by nature in times when man had not, to the same extent, shaken off natural restrictions, this does not of course mean that these natural ties have completely ceased or become simply irrelevant. This new service of protecting defenseless man can, indeed, consist precisely in re-forming such natural ties, now that they have ceased to be taken for granted, intelligently cultivating them, and achieving a new understanding and a free, responsible acceptance of them by man. The new service may consist (this is perhaps one of its most important tasks) in bringing it about that nature in a conscious, cultivated, cared-for form shall reign where before there was simply nature as something taken for granted, and today there is destructive un-nature.

But here, too, what we have been saying stands: much of what used to be simply forcibly imposed by nature has got to continue today and be made new by the chosen, responsible, free act of man himself. Much of what used to be taken for granted and indisputable is going to be in daily need of being achieved afresh and constructed afresh. Much of what used to be preserved simply by institutional forces is only going to remain in a healthy state if it is under the protection of a continual free decision, rising up from the heart at each moment as a grace of God. Hence the whole dignity of this service, and the burden of it. The only impression that this service can produce today is the oppressive sense that it is always all to be begun again, that there is no getting beyond the beginning, that nothing can be built up any more so as to stand on its own without the support of fervently loving hearts. This is why this new service is so difficult, so much a matter of hoping against hope; this is why it continually demands the uttermost energies from the poor hearts that often seem to themselves so empty, weary and weak. This is why, ultimately, anchoring it institutionally in laws, rules, regulations by the State, etc., does not really help, useful and necessary as all these things can be, and much as we have to strive to get them done. This is why we can no longer, to the same extent as in earlier times, build the future of Christianity on what is provided and what is handed down, on custom and tradition. This is why, in the end, the only thing that is any protection today is the greater love of a heart made strong in God.

When we confess that Jesus Christ became man and suffered for us men and for our salvation, we are at the same
time clearly stating that the Church is not an end in herself
but exists for men. But this also means that the service of
which we are speaking, as the new task of the Church and of
Christians in a new situation, really is a service of men. It has
to come to rest in them, and not turn back towards itself. I
mean that this service contributes most to the growth of
Christianity, which is the religion of self-forgetful love, when
it thinks about *people themselves:* each one of them, all of
them, those far off as well as those near, the unhappy creature
from whom there is nothing to be gained, who is no addition
to the battalions of the Church Militant, as much as the
people who will subsequently vote Christian Democrat. In
an age of misdirected welfare, of a statism that uses welfare
bureaucracy as a means of bullying men, an age in which man
perishes even though he is better fed than in earlier times,
the more we can convince a person, in deed and in truth, that
we are serving him because we love him in God and are
seeking for nothing besides, the more we shall convince him
of Christ, of God's grace and love in the community of those
who love, which is the Church. They can take a great deal
away from us Christians, but not this love, because they could
only take this by taking it into their own hearts. But this can
only be done by a Christian. Mere charitable activity does
not recruit men to the Church and to Christianity, any more
than State welfare engenders love of one's country. But it is
not some modern theory, worked out just now for the purpose
of a jubilee speech, it is the gospel that says that real divine
caritas is a power of God, which can bring conviction of the
truth of the gospel. There would be no use in having the

churches open if the railway missions were closed. The gateway into the Church is the pierced heart of the Lord and of those who share in his destiny of sacrificial love. One who thus works by love to draw men to truth, because the ultimate truth is the God who is love, will often sow only for another to reap, and often sow his seeds with tears, working in hope for the future. But he needs to be convinced that his way is at least as important as any other that can be followed for the spread of Christianity and the winning of genuine conviction of the divine origin of Jesus' message.

I must finish. As you see, I have not said very much of a practical nature. But I can surely trust that your working conference is going to provide for you fully in this respect. But though it has not been practical, what has been said was an attempt to set in a wide context the aims and work of the association now celebrating its jubilee. That context is really the one great all-embracing task of the Church towards eternal humanity, the old task in a new age at whose threshold we stand. But the fact that there are associations like this one, which saw and accepted this new service right at the beginning of the new age, gives us a pledge that the new age, too, belongs to God and his Christ as a time of salvation, throughout every process of decline and resurgence. We are pilgrims, all of us, on the road. At the end of all our pilgrimages we shall meet with those who were journeying too, whom we met on the roads and railways of the world and in the canyon-like streets of great cities. We shall meet those who travelled with us the uncharted, self-determined roads of the new humanity, chosen not by protective nature but by the divine and demonic freedom of man himself. And we shall be asked by God whether we have travelled with these others in an association of love, whether we have been concerned about them, whether we have taken them under the protection of our love, so that all these roads may lead, for them too, into the infinite freedom and glory of God.

Note

[1] The German word "Elend" formerly meant "abroad, foreign parts" (cf. "Ausland"). It now means "wretchedness, misery." (Tr.)

3
Parish and Place of Work

"The world has changed" is the title of a book by Eberhard
Müller on current problems of Protestant pastoral theology.
Among the many changes with which pastoral work has got
to reckon (which apply equally to the Catholics of Germany),
there is one to which we shall devote some attention here:
the shift in the "location" of pastoral work. It is not that
E. Müller is the first to have seen the phenomenon in question.[1] But he sees it clearly and formulates it sharply. We
cannot refrain from quoting a few sentences at least:

> Passing away of the local community. The third great
> change which has taken place has been in the structure of
> human society. The classical structure with its levels of
> family, community, nation and state is no longer able
> today to account for more than a part of real life. Group-
> ings according to profession have a much stronger co-
> hesive power. In country areas, the great factories have
> much more sociological importance than the ties of
> locality. But the Church's work, in her ministry and
> organization, is exclusively orientated to the old social
> structure. The parochial ministry confines itself to ap-
> proaching people according to the old sociological group-
> ings, overlooking the fact that it is thus addressing itself

solely to the world of home and family (p. 13). . . .
The Church will certainly not be in a position to make
this missionary advance into the world of work as it
exists today unless she gives up her completely one-sided
misplacement of the bulk of her work onto the care of
local communities. True, there is an orientation of missionary work to the local community which is ultimately
valid for all times and not to be abandoned. . . . But we
must recognize the fact that today completely new communities have arisen in between the local communities,
so to speak, and are receiving no care from the Church:
the living communities which are factories and other
collectives based on work. Since the members of these
communities do not as a rule come from one locality, but
gravitate together each morning from a number of local
communities, an advance into this world of work cannot
take place within the limits of Church parishes as they
are today . . . (p. 29).

We see that their difficulties and tasks are the same as ours,
and the fact that they see them should be a further spur to
us not to overlook them. Attempts to focus on this displace-
ment of the context of pastoral work and to draw conclusions
from it have not been totally lacking. One such attempt,[2]
and a very promising one, consists in the Catholic Betriebsmännerwerke and the Christian Werkgemeinschaften (the
first name is current in the Northwest, the second in the South,
which does not necessarily imply that the two words mean
exactly the same thing). As a very loose description, what
they mean is that people belonging to the same concern come
together with the idea of helping each other and consulting

and working together to carry out the apostolic duties and missionary tasks which a layman, as a true Christian, has in his place of work. The Cardinal of Cologne, speaking at the first general conference of the Catholic Betriebsmännerwerke in the Landtag building in Düsseldorf on October 25th, 1953, said: "To take religious hold on men in the place where their interest is concentrated, where they spend the greater part of their life—this is a splendid idea." It is not proposed here to give a closer description of these groups in industry or an account of their foundation, dissemination and work in Germany or in other countries. What is offered here is simply a few considerations of principle on the basis of the meaning and value of such groups, and hence on the limitations of the parochial principle.

The fact that such Christian groups exist gives rise in a new way to the question "*To whom* is the gospel message of salvation actually addressed, who is the recipient of its truth and its grace?" The answer is, of course, ultimately, "The individual human being, each individual in all nations and all ages." For each is a person, with his own unique responsibility which no one can take away from him, each, in freedom, says his yes or no to God. But this is not the sense in which the question is meant here; or, better: it should not be thought that this is the whole answer. For however unique as a person each individual is, he is also a member of numerous communities and associations; and all language, including the preaching of the gospel, precisely presupposes this social character in man as something there to be addressed. The question is thus "*Which* community, *which* social pattern, is the one in which the Christian message comes seeking for men?" For it is beyond doubt that this message does not

only *make* him a member of a new community, the Church
as a whole and the individual liturgical community: it sees
him from the start as a creature who is not absolutely isolated. Hence we can ask, *"Where* does the message seek out
human beings for their redemption?"

Historical Observations

Let us try to find an answer to this question first by making
a few historical observations and then through certain theo-
retical considerations. If we look at the New Testament, we
notice an interesting thing. The missionary work of the apostolic age was in the highest degree flexible, unscrupulously
flexible, one might almost say, in making use of every conceivable sociological point of contact for reaching human
beings and offering them Christian salvation. We must not
naively imagine that, because all men are called to salvation,
the missions of the apostolic age had as their goal only separate individuals in their isolation. Naturally, when Paul
preached at a street corner or in a public square, his audience
was Everyman: anyone and everyone who happened to pass
by and stop there; i.e. the atomized urban human being. But
when he preached in the synagogue, the sociological milieu
which he *took for granted* was a community with a formed
outlook on life, composed of born Jews and of Gentiles who
were already Jewish proselytes. When a "house," with all
its servants, followed the example of its master or mistress
in becoming Christian, then the sociological basis of Paul's
missionary success was the *natural* community of family and
household. When he rented a public hall to give "lectures,"
this enterprise was directed, sociologically speaking, to that

particular educational level which could be reached by such lectures.

Behind the primitive community in Jerusalem, which still felt itself as almost like a sect or (more accurately, perhaps) a kind of higher brotherhood within the official Jewish Church, we can, in part, guess at the existence of similar brotherhoods which, as a higher religious milieu, would have formed the best recruiting ground for the first Christians. Again, in the primitive Jerusalem community we can see the two sociological groups from which it was recruited, Hebrews and Hellenists.

Thus, however variegated in their composition, the apostolic communities in Judea and amongst the Gentiles may have been, being made up of slaves, artisans, sailors, dockers, merchants, shopkeepers, minor officials and those few Christians who came from higher social strata—householder, proconsul, a few representatives of the Jewish religious leaders (priests, rulers of synagogues)—yet this fact does not mean that the missionary work of the apostolic age was aimed simply at the mass of human beings regarded as a multitude of individuals. These missions did not only *construct* communities but presupposed human association as their starting-point, and (this is the decisive point) to such an extent that all associations were welcome so long as they made it possible to approach the individual. The result of this is, indeed, the *local church*, but it is not really the local community that is the starting-point of missionary work. The starting-point presupposed by the local church was not the atomized individual, either, but innumerable different sociological structures, distinct from the local community, which formed the natural basis for the supernatural community of Christians in the

Church. Paul's great missionary achievement is not only that, theologically, he no longer addressed himself exclusively to the Jews but also that, at the practical level, he recognized, besides the religious basis of the synagogue community, other sociological bases, on which it was possible to reach the Gentiles.

During the succeeding period, with the Church working amongst peoples who had, as a whole, been Christianized, it was of course almost exclusively the *local community* which was the sociological basis for preaching and pastoral work, and the parish, as a territorial unit, was practically the only form taken by the individual community of faithful. In reference to the individual church, "church" and parish or diocese became almost synonymous, which does not by any means necessarily follow in principle from the nature of the individual Christian community. But even from post-apostolic times down to our own day, the sociological starting-points for the Church's activity and the effect of it in the shape of a church community have not been exclusively of a territorial nature, i.e. local community and parish respectively. If we examine it closely, the parish church of the early Middle Ages belonged equally to locality and to place of *work;* it was a church for those belonging to one manor, so that its basis was economic and not merely territorial. When a monastic community had its own pastor this meant that here a religious brotherhood was the basis for the actual ecclesiastical community and its pastoral functions. The fact that the medieval guilds were also something in the nature of religious confraternities meant that here an association with an economic aim was set athwart the local community as a basis for the religious strivings and Christian instruction of its members. Court chaplains, army chaplains, university chaplaincies, religious services and instruction in schools, special pastoral provision for national minorities and other types of "personal parish," private oratories, household chapels, the apostolate of the wandering apostles in the early Church (alongside the established local clergy) and of the wandering Celtic monks of the early Middle Ages, pastoral work by monasteries and medieval mendicant orders, pastoral work for particular social groups by modern orders in the post-Tridentine Church, third orders, congregations, the Oratorians, pilgrimage churches and the pastoral work done through pilgrimages—all these phenomena and others besides show that the Church's mission has never simply moved between the local community and the local parish as its beginning and its end, that besides the territorial basis there have always been other sociological facts forming the natural foundation for Christian communities, for "a church" and its apostolate.

We will add here (without trying to prove it in detail) that modern Canon Law does not by any means confine itself to recognizing the parochial principle, so as to make the territorial principle the one exclusive basic norm for the formation of the community and the building up of pastoral work.[3] The Church's theory, like her practice, recognizes not only the principle of locality but also that of social grouping and of freely formed groups—religious associations within the Church, that is, which are based not on the common residence but the common status or profession of their members, or on freely chosen association. It is not of any immediate importance whether, in these cases, the persons concerned also belong to a local parish or not. For even if they do, it is still true that there are religious communities in the Church

whose basis is not common residence and territorial neighborhood. Hence we discern the "federal principle" in pastoral
and apostolic work, as a combination of the principles of status
association and free association, and also (to state it without
further ado) the principle of the work-community as a combination of the professional (and status) principle and the
territorial principle.

Considerations of Principle

Let us now add some considerations of principle to these historical indications. Parishes and dioceses exist, not because of
something in the supernatural character of the Church as
such, but because the Church addresses herself to human
beings, and human beings are localized beings, naturally apt
to be at home somewhere, with a local neighborhood; and
hence a religious community made up of human beings, in
the visible, concrete form that it takes in history, cannot but
accept this kind of natural, human association as the substruc-
ture of its own ecclesiastical community. But this being so, it
must also be said that in whatever way, in whatever degree,
in whatever intensity *any* social factor is one of the forces
determining human life it can, in that same way, degree and
intensity, be a natural point of entry for the Church's missionary approach and a natural foundation for forming a
Christian community and for the apostolic activity of individual Christians. Because and in so far as people inevitably
belong to several, and internally diverse, natural communities,
it is not a mark of pastoral chaos, but an obvious necessity
arising out of the nature of man and his links with different

communities, when they also belong to a number of different (clearly not all equally important) religious communities. An exclusive organization of pastoral and apostolic work by the parish would have to be based on the notion that the one and only naturally significant and hence religiously important association of human beings is that of the local neighborhood. But this notion, which has to be presupposed if the parochial principle is to be made exclusive, is simply false. Man as a social being belongs to his local neighborhood, to his particular professional grouping, to his particular cultural level, to his particular national group (which need not in all circumstances necessarily coincide with a given territory), to associations freely entered into, to groups formed according to age and sex, to groups formed by a common experience. All these social relationships and many others can have their importance as providing occasion for the formation of groups to which the Church's message and teaching mission can be explicitly addressed; which can, according to circumstances, be the foundation of "communities" in the theological sense; and which can also be the immediate context for the exercise of the individual Christian's apostolic responsibility.

We must now set the community of one's place of work in this framework of history and principle.

The Working Community as an Object of Pastoral Care

We can begin by stating in principle that if and in so far as the work-community really is a community, it can, according to the theological principles just expounded, be in principle the natural basis of an ecclesiastical religious community in the threefold sense in which we have been considering all such communities so far: as that to which the Church addresses the missionary work of her hierarchical, priestly apostolate; as an individual community in the Church; and as a field for the apostolate of the individual Christian aware of his human and Christian responsibility, of his royal priesthood in respect of his brothers. Now, a place of work is a genuine community; or rather, to speak more circumspectly: despite all the sinful inadequacy and distortion that there is in all human institutions, his real, concrete entity does still embody the essential character, belonging to the natural law and the order of creation, of a human community of work. For man is obliged to work, and all human work is ultimately co-operation, a contribution to the life of the community, outside which no human being can live, physically or mentally. There has to be a community of work, because of the very nature of man. To the extent to which a concern is fulfilling a valid task of this kind within the community of the nation, the state, and mankind, in respect of a morally lawful end, it is a true community of work and hence can be a natural entity in the order of salvation capable of being, in its fashion, just as much as the territorial neighborhood (though in a different way and without itself becoming exclusive), the natural basis for a religious participation in the Church as a whole.

There are two further considerations to add:

1. The modern territorial neighborhood, the natural basis of the parish (and the diocese), simply does not coincide any more with the neighborhood in the sense which used to provide the basis of the parish. The parish used to be sociologically patterned on the kind of neighborhood represented by the village and the country town. So long as this will not

be taken as denigration of the parish (including the modern parish), and remembering that the religious community as such is not to be confused with its natural basis, it needs to be clearly and honestly said that the parish in a great modern city (as regards its basis, not itself) is patterned on an urban police area, not on the kind of territorial neighborhood found in a village or country town. The latter is not simply an area of common residence, which is almost all there is in a great city today, but contains other communal elements as well. It used to be almost identical with the place of work, and was also the place of recreation, entertainment and education; it was bound together by ties of kindred; it could be personally experienced and seen as a whole through acquaintanceship, communal celebrations, etc.; it was not so atomized by freedom of movement as is the case today. In other words, a parish in a large town (and to a growing extent in the country as well) simply does not possess its former attributes any longer. The communities of work and of locality used in practice to coincide; this is no longer the case. So the Church is faced with the choice: *either* to confine herself to building her religious communities on local communities, now reduced almost to mere police districts (and cherish utopian hopes that this reduction in the natural basis for ecclesiastical community can be compensated for by supernatural, community-building forces[4]); *or* to go along with the process of disintegration now happening to natural communities and seek out the community of work (as being an important basis for religious community) where it is now to be found—outside the local neighborhood, in the factory or office.

2. Modern concerns cannot avoid being communities, and they endeavor to strengthen their community life, humaniz-

ing it and extending it beyond the sphere of mere production. We are not here concerned in the first instance either to justify this development or to point out its dangers and limitations. We are concerned simply with the fact. Given that the place of work is in fact a community which to an ever increasing degree—rightly or wrongly, a blessing or a disaster —does absorb human life into itself, then the pastoral, religious importance of such a community is bound to grow. Even if this growth in the work community is a danger, it must in any case mean an increase in its importance as the sociological basis for building a Christian community.

The whole of this discussion so far has amounted only to these two points: (a) The formation of the Christian community never rests only on the isolated individual on the one hand and the community-forming power of Christian truth and grace, on the sacraments and the cult, on the other; it is also sustained by natural communities. As to the question of what natural communities can be considered as this kind of basis, the practice and doctrine of the Church have always maintained that the community of the local neighborhood is not the only community that can form such a basis. (b) Amongst the various possible alternative communities capable of being that to which the Church's mission is addressed, of sustaining a religious community life, and of being the context for individual apostolic action, the place of work holds an important position, once it becomes impossible for the parish to be, universally, what it once was, because of the profound changes that have affected its natural basis.

Thus it follows from what has been said that alongside the parochial principle there does exist the "place-of-work principle": the pastoral norm that the place of work can, and in certain circumstances must, be considered as a sociological setting for pastoral care along with the place of residence (the basis of the parish). This "place-of-work principle" is a norm combining the professional principle and the principle of place (place not meaning simply place of residence), in so far as an industrial or business concern is both a spatial and a professional unit. In so far as a Christian group in such a concern is a freely formed association, it can also appeal as a justification for its existence to the "free-group principle": the norm that groups formed from below by free association can also be the object of the Church's preaching and pastoral care (e.g. youth groups). For it is not the case that associations can only be the object of pastoral care in the Church when they have been brought into being from above, founded by the hierarchy.[5]

We must now speak of the limitations of the "place-of-work principle," which has now been established as a concrete application of the professional and local principles combined, with the right to take its place alongside the "parochial principle" in the building up of the community of the Church.

Limits of the "Place-of-Work Principle"

It is clear, in the first place, that a community based on the place of work, rightly understood, cannot be a replacement for or a restriction on the parish, and would not try to be. In terms both of Church history and of Canon Law, the parish is *"in possessione."* The parish is founded on the very same basic fact from which we have deduced the "place-of-work principle": the fact that an ecclesiastical, religious community has its material basis in a natural community. However real-

istic we have to be in recognizing that the residential neighborhood, the basis of the parish, has declined in importance
as an element in the life of modern urban man, it still remains
true, even today, that it retains enough human significance
and practical usefulness as a community to make the parish
that is built upon it an irreplaceable necessity. One might well,
perhaps, go on from this to an account of what it can and
ought to provide, and what it ought to recognize itself as
unsuited or incompetent to do. But this is not the place for it.
It is easily seen that the Christian associations in work communities, in the form in which they are in fact functioning,
are not in competition with the parishes: so long, that is, as
the latter do not have an exaggerated idea of their own
potentialities; or strain the parochial principle to the point
of laying claim, beyond their competence, to a pastoral and
religious monopoly; or undervalue and play down the tasks
and potentialities of missionary initiatives on the part of the
Church or the individual Christian, simply because they cannot fall within the scope of the parish itself.[6]

So long as we can count on there being as much objectivity
and public spirit amongst the various kinds of pastor (secular
and regular clergy, parish clergy and group chaplaincies) as
is taken for granted, for instance, in the relations between
doctor and clinic, general practitioner and specialist, then no
insuperable difficulties can arise about drawing the practical
lines between different pastoral activities within the one
Church. So long as every pastor is ready and willing to do
anything that calls for sacrifice and unselfishness and to leave
to someone else what that someone else can do better than
he; so long as no one imagines it to be beneath his dignity
to admit that it is not possible to be a specialist in everything

(there being many things which can only be done by special-
ists), then the various "principles" of pastoral theology will
never become the battle-cries of warring pastors.

But there is still another limitation which needs to be men-
tioned on the place-of-work principle in the Church's pastoral
and missionary work. The pastoral and missionary significance
of the place-of-work principle depends on the human significance of the place of work. But that significance is variable,
fluid, and, precisely in our present situation, a matter of dispute. The attempt is being made today, in a different way
from formerly, to make the concern for which one works in
a sense one's home: health service, meals, use of free time,
holidays, social intercourse, care of small children in day-
nurseries, further education, etc., are all being put on this
basis. Thus there is an effort going on to make such a concern
a community embracing and including the whole of human
life. What lies behind this may not be only a praiseworthy
effort (praiseworthy even if perhaps mistaken in some of its
methods and overstepping justified limits) to humanize industry and its organization; an effort of this kind may also
represent, consciously or unconsciously, the aim of devaluing
human beings by reducing them, in all fields, to mere functions of technical work and technical success. It would never
be permissible for a pastor in industry to further such an
aim. It would be a reversal of every true order of values. Such
a pastor is not a psychological technician, an expert in industrial mental hygiene, with the job of preventing any falling-
off in production through spiritual conflicts amongst the
workers. It must be clearly understood in any Christian association in industry and in its activities that work is for God,
not religion for work. It must be clear that, when it comes

to the orientation of the whole of human life, the industrial concern as such cannot be the primary and ultimate norm; that it would, ultimately, be a capitalistic or communistic inhumanity for such a concern to try to swallow up first work, home, recreation, neighborhood, sport, health service, and then go on to mental life and freedom of association, and finally to the Church and religion, so as to make them subordinate functions of itself. Any advance in the idea of industrial association has got to lead to a humanization of work, not to a still greater dehumanization of men. And it is only in so far as a concern is serving this right aim, or at least not opposing it, that it can serve as the basis and context of the Church's missionary work.

There is a third essential limitation on the place-of-work principle to which attention needs to be drawn. A Catholic Betriebsmännerwerk—a group of Catholics working in some concern—is, indeed, a society of laymen, but one with a specifically Christian objective. Only if it has this task clearly in focus will it avoid the danger of accomplishing nothing by trying everything. It follows that a Catholic association of this kind is not directly a vehicle for activities and tasks that are economic, socio-political or otherwise secular in content. These tasks are a matter of Christian responsibility, must be carried out in a Christian fashion, and are liable to be built into an unchristian way of life; hence the Catholic group can and should do all in its power to ensure that these tasks and activities are seen in a Christian spirit and carried out by well-instructed Christians. But it cannot itself directly be the vehicle for such tasks. If this is observed, there will be no room for legitimate conflict between such Catholic groups and the works councils, trade unions and similar institutions to whom this secular task does directly belong and which are really its immediate vehicles.

It follows from this too that when Christians in the same concern have a human, Christian and apostolic fellow-feeling with one another, and work together as Christians, despite their different types of job in the concern and their different social positions, this does not have for its purpose the further-ance of romantic paternalism. Christians everywhere are cer-tainly meant to meet each other in a spirit of patience, readi-ness to understand, self-criticism, justice and love, and so to work out their differences of opinion, wage disputes, etc. And how much would be accomplished if this were to become more and more the case! But it would be an unchristian error, an heretical denial of the contingency and profound disorder and sinfulness of this world, to suppose that, given a little good will, all conflicts and all use of force are avoid-able, at least against anyone whose convictions are sincere and who must be supposed to be of good will. When we say that Christians are against the class struggle, this means that we deny that brute force and power ought to have the last word or are capable on their own of achieving justice. But it does not mean that every kind of force, i.e. use of power, by which anything is achieved without the free and willing consent of the other side is necessarily and always an injustice, or that the application of force to differences of opinion on social questions can always be avoided. So a Catho-lic group in an industrial concern brings people of different social levels together in a spirit of Christian love and hu-manity. But it in no way prohibits a worker who is a member of such a group, in a case in which his Christian conscience and his own just interests, properly understood, require

it of him (e.g. in a wage dispute), from siding without qualification with his trade union and joining with it in the fight
for a wage increase. A society of apostolic Christians aware
of their missionary responsibilities has nothing to do with
an outworn paternalism.

Even with all these essential limitations to be observed,
the Christian groups in industrial concerns still retain their
significance. For today, such a concern is an area of life which
simply cannot, as in former times, be taken care of purely by
other communities. It has made the place of work spatially
and organizationally self-sufficient; hence it must either remain something formless in terms of Christianity, making it
a permanent source of danger to Christian life, or else it must
be given its own Christian formation as such, through a community appropriate to itself: a society of the Christians working in it.

Notes

[1] The literature on these problems has become very extensive of
recent years. Cf., the present author's "Peaceful Reflections on the
Parochial Principle" in *Theological Investigations*, vol. 2, London
(1963), pp. 283-318; J. Höffner, "Um das Pfarrprinzip," *Trierer
Theologische Zeitschrift*, 56 (1947), pp. 60-2; O. von Nell-Breuning,
"Pfarrgemeinde, Pfarrfamilie, Pfarrprinzip," *Trierer Theologische
Zeitschrift*, 56 (1947), pp. 257-62; J. Höffner, "Nochmals das
Pfarrprinzip," *ibid.*, 57 (1948), pp. 236-9; A. Schrott, *Seelsorge im
Wandel der Zeiten. Formen und Organisation seit der Begründung des
Pfarrinstituts*, Graz (1949); M. Marchi, *Esperienze parrocchiali*, Rome
(1949); A. Kirchgässner, *Pfarrgemeinde und Pfarrgottesdienst*, Frei-
burg (1949); C. Noppel, *Aedificatio corporis Christi*, 2nd ed., Freiburg
(1949); K. Lechner, *Laie und Pfarre*, Vienna (1949); R. Perenna,
Innovazioni o rinnovamento della parrocchia? Como (1950); B.
Socche, *La communità parrocchiale*, Rome (1950); A. Ryckmans, *La*

paroisse vivante, Tournai (1950): G. Viviani, *La parroquia*, Rome (1950); H. Légaré, *Introduction à la sociologie paroissiale*, Lille (1950); J. Miller, "Beiträge zum Pfarrprinzip," *Orientierung*, 15 (1951), p. 163; B. Benz, "Die neuen französischen Seelsorgsmethoden und ihre Bedeutung für Deutschland," *Tübinger Theologische Quartalschrift*, 131 (1951), pp. 208-47, 320-39, 464-86; L. Borlée, "Structures sociales et ministère paroissial," *Rev. Dioc. Tournai*, 6 (1951), pp. 427-46; J. Peitzmeier, "Jugendgruppenarbeit und Jugendpsychologie," *Theologie und Glaube*, 42 (1952), pp. 454-61 (an important evaluation of parochial youth work); R. Spiazzi, "Spunti per una teologia della parrocchia," *Scuola Catt.*, 80 (1952), pp. 26-42; A. Schrott, "Pfarrseelsorge und überpfarrliche Seelsorge," *Der Seelsorger*, 23 (1953), pp. 202-8; P. Virton, *Enquêtes de sociologie paroissiale*, Paris (1953); *Die Pfarre, Gestalt und Sendung*, Vienna (1953); *La Maison-Dieu*, 36, vol. 4 (1953), "Problèmes de la Paroisse." There are also numerous references over the years in *Herder-Korrespondenz*.

[2] Only an attempt. Pastoral work in a factory might well, for instance, be done independently of any Betriebsmännerwerk, a word which denoted primarily a group of apostolically active *laymen*. Here and there pastoral beginnings and attempts are being made through "factory chaplains." Thus the basic reflections offered here could well form the starting-point for more far-reaching demands. But because the Catholic Betriebsmännerwerke are, in our country, the most obvious embodiment of reflections of this kind, we are making them our basis.

[3] See the articles listed above by the present author and by O. von Nell-Breuning.

[4] Things said about the "parish family" seem to contain something of that optimism which can easily become utopian: the idea that supernatural community forces can take the place of the natural "village family," which was the basis of the "parish family" in a village but is simply not available any more in a large town.

[5] Cf. my essay "Peaceful Reflections" in *Theological Investigations*, vol. 2, especially pp. 302-6.

[6] E. Müller, quoted above, writes: "The place of the old social structures of the community as mediating institutions is being taken by the community of the place of work, the professional association, the sports ground, and other forms of community experience. So far, the Church has taken scarcely any account of this factual change. Indeed, there is even discernible, in many quarters, a growing defensiveness on the part of the parochial clergy against the so-called 'confraternity

jungle' (men's societies, women's societies, youth councils, the Evangelical Academy, and so on), which is understood as including everything not confined in its activities within the parochial limits of a residential area . . ." (p. 14). Nevertheless, the whole third section of Müller's little book is devoted to "Revitalizing the Local Community" (pp. 35-47).

4

The Prison Pastorate

You, who are prison chaplains, have come together here for an hour's meditation as priests. The meaning of such an hour can precisely *not* be to think out how the charge laid upon you is to be made fruitful and beneficial for those entrusted to your care, but must be directed to considering how such a pastor with such a charge is himself to find God. This does not mean that the task of caring selflessly for others, and Christian neighborly love itself, are being changed into egotism. We are merely giving scope to the simple, fundamental insight that in our priestly lives we can only serve others in so far as we are ourselves filled with the grace of him to whom we are bearing witness, and whom we are there to mediate to men in his word, his sacraments and his grace. Nor is anything changed in this either by our objective official mission or by the power of the *opus operatum*. For both of these have got to be accepted by men if they are to be effective. But they will be accepted only if those who bring them are such as to make their objective mission and objective grace credible by the quality of their own Christian living. Nor can we simply say that selfless service is itself holy, and that the more a person forgets himself in it and dies to himself, the more he will be filled with the grace of God and the more be apt to win his neighbor by the witness of the Spirit and of power. In its positive sense, this statement is true. But it would turn into a dangerous lie if we supposed that it could provide the one single all-embracing norm for our mission. There are no maxims in the spiritual life capable of providing, on their own, a total formula covering the whole thing. There is no way of including everything in one exercise. For we are creatures who, even in this respect, have no abiding city, but must humbly, in our finitude, do many different things in order to reach the whole. So we have got to take pains over our own nearness to God if we are to be able to serve our neighbor, and we draw near to God *by* serving our neighbor: each depends on the other, and yet they are not both the same thing. And that is why, in an hour of meditation such as this, it is our task and our office themselves which bid us take to heart our concern over our own salvation in the midst of our task.

What we shall be considering during this short meditation can be summed up in two sentences. In the prisoners entrusted to our pastoral care we find Christ our Lord; and in these prisoners we find ourselves, what we see in them being the concealed truth of our own situation.

Christ in the Prisoners

We find Christ our Lord in the prisoners. We have got to find him there; he is really there to be found, and to be found in such a way that our encounter with him will also be for our salvation and our happiness.

There is no need for me to remind you of your own experience as prison chaplains. This experience, in all its bitterness and horrible realism, is more present to you than anything

I could describe or suggest of it: the experience of shattered human existences; the mental and moral defectives; the unstable characters; the psychopaths; the vicious, the smooth, the cynical, the hypocrites and liars; the merely impulsive, the victims of circumstances, of addiction, the inevitable recidivists, the religiously impervious, the poor devils, the imbeciles. Even though this kind of experience is not the only one that you have in prisons, even though you also meet people there who strike you immediately as no different from anyone else—normal, decent men—yet it still remains true that you have often been struck with horror by the humanity you encounter there. You have so often been let down, shown up as stupid, rewarded with ingratitude; so often knocked in vain for admission to hearts that were locked and barred; so often provided help only to be rejected as yourselves representatives of the hated system. You have suffered the sense of futility and the hopelessness of all such efforts; you must often have had the impression that all your efforts, your concern, your love, your patience and your work are being dropped into a bottomless abyss from which no response ever comes. You are men who continually encounter evil in all its dreary, nerve-racking, hopeless, detestable reality. You know all that better than I do. And now let us read the words of Christ, his incredible, provocative, thrilling words: "Come, ye blessed of my Father, possess you the kingdom prepared for you from the foundation of the world. . . . For I was in prison, and you came to me. . . . Then shall the just answer him, saying: Lord, when did we see thee in prison, and came to thee? And the king answering, shall say to them: Amen I say to you, as long as you did it to one of these my least brethren, you did it to me" (Mt. 25, 34-40).

I think that the first thing for you to do is simply to rejoice over these words. They apply to you without any kind of translation, just as they were spoken then. They do not need to be translated and adapted and transposed into a new set of circumstances. What you live is a primary, abiding form of life which Jesus saw clearly in its abiding pattern; he gives it expression in a statement which he then raises to the level of a concrete utterance of God's judgment, the judgment which brings world history to its fulfillment, treads out as in a winepress the ultimate meaning of that history, and transforms it into the wine of eternal joy. There are few vocations with such words to rejoice over, few that find themselves being addressed in so unchanged a fashion by the mouth of the Son of Man with words at once realistically human and divinely heavenly.

But the next response to these words has to be one of terror: you are commanded to find our Lord in these people whom you visit in prison. What a terrifying and exacting task! Do not say that these words are not meant to be taken quite so seriously as that. Do not say that all that is really wanted when you get right down to it, is a little human compassion, a certain amount of reasonably allocated help; some of the sober realism which has no illusions but at the same time is not too ready to despair of humanity: which has the humanist optimism to believe in the good in every human being, stimulate it and give it another chance to do better; and which, when that fails, consoles itself with the thought that after all there are psychopathic conditions which can be as incurable as other diseases and ought not to break one's heart any more than the others: the patients all die in the end anyway, but the human race doesn't let itself get excessively depressed over it. No, no and again no. More is asked of you than this.

You are to find our Lord in these prisoners. You yourselves are to encounter him there to your own saving benefit. Are we not under the temptation to ask our Lord, impatiently and (as we like to see it) unsentimentally, in the name of sober realism, reason and our own experience, "When did we see you in prison?" Are we not tempted to say, "We were in the prisons, but we didn't find you there?—We found pitiful human beings, poor devils and cynical criminals. But you? No, not you."

Perhaps we shall say: "We've nothing against it if you like to be so magnanimous and gracious as to use a sort of splendid heavenly fiction to count these services rendered, these visits to the prison, *as if* we had done them to you. That's all right, that's fine, we have no objection to a fiction of that sort. But a fiction it remains. You are you and these people are these people. And we did not find you in the prisons. Not there, of all places."

But Jesus says otherwise. Jesus rejects all our realism as unreal. He does not identify himself with these people by a legal fiction, but in such a way that we are, in very truth, encountering him in them. We have got to let his words stand as what they are. And believe them. We can think about *how* they can be true, but we have got to take them as true. We can be horrified at how little we must have grasped of the self-emptying love of God in Christ, the *agape* of God, if we have not understood that there really is a love in this world— the love of God, that is—which accepts when, to us, it seems that there is no longer anything there to be accepted; a love which is not a matter of gracious condescension but truly, in all reality and effectiveness, identifies itself with these sinners; a love which strips itself, exposes itself, commits itself, spends itself utterly; in which the lover can no longer find himself except in and through the beloved. We can consider the truths that this love is creative and transforming; that it is genuine and radical even to death, the death of the cross; that it has dared to descend into the uttermost emptiness of God-forsaken, death-stricken lovelessness and has there been victorious and taken all things to itself; that it is a love which brought the Son of God to make himself a curse that he might really save what is really and inescapably lost—that which is, of itself, dead, without future and without hope; that which grimly locks and bars itself against all love; that which, with cold contempt and unambiguous cynicism, scorns love, purity, kindliness and loyalty as utopian pretense.

It is with such sinners that this love has, in strict reality, identified itself. For otherwise they would not be redeemed. Otherwise, only what is sound in itself would have been saved (whereas no such thing exists, though it often seems to; so that we think that this thing, basically good in itself, has been accepted by God because it is good, instead of believing that what was truly lost has been accepted in order that it should be made good). We must think about the truth, accepting it in faith and against our own "experience," that the Lord is in these lost individuals whom we meet in the prisons: that he is in them by his will to love, which calls nothingness and that which is lost by its name and creates it; in them by his patience, by the almighty power that sees, even in this bit of the wreckage of world history, a person, an eternity, a brother of the incarnate Word of God, a beloved, someone to be taken seriously with divine seriousness: sees him as this, or, better, creates him as this by looking on him with love. HE is, in all truth, in them; because the primary mystery of that love which creates and makes one, which *is* God himself, is not understood, and hence the essence of Christianity is radically misunderstood, unless this improbable, paradoxical truth, with its radical reversal of all our shortsighted experience, is unconditionally accepted in faith.

But if we want to understand our Lord's words and find him in the prisoners, we must not only think, in faith and prayer, about the truth that he is in them; we must think even more about how we can find him in them. For this is the appalling thing, the deadly danger: that we can fail to recognize him, even though he is in these lost, unfortunate brothers of his, one with them. We are liable to pass him by; our eyes can be held, our hearts be dull and closed against him, so that we do not see him. In this time of faith and not of sight we shall indeed never find him except in a hidden fashion. When the last day comes, we shall still be among those who ask wonderingly, just as much as those who have not visited the Lord and not found him, "When did we see thee in prison, and came to thee?" (Mt. 25, 39, 44). As far as *experience* goes it will always be like this. It will seem to us that it is not he, that it is not possible to find him in the prisoners. But this is precisely what Christianity is, this finding when we think we have not found, this seeing when we seem to be gazing into darkness, this having when we think that we have lost. And so it is here. We have to seek and find him in the prisoners. And it is not easy. It is possible to ignore him and walk blindly past him even when you are there in the prisons with your bodily presence and your

"carrying out of your duties," even when you have the repu-
tation of being a good prison chaplain.

What does it mean to find Christ himself in his brothers
in prison? First and foremost, it means a reverent humility
in face of this other human being, who is a child of God and
a brother of Jesus Christ, one who is called and beloved by
God, one who is embraced by the power of divine love. We
all know (and anyone who denied it would be at the very
least a Jansenist heretic, doubting God's universal will to
save) that every human being still on pilgrimage through
this life is called to salvation, beloved of God, and embraced
by the grace of Christ, even if he has not yet freely accepted
it. We know that we cannot ultimately judge anybody, that we
cannot say of anybody with absolute certainty that he is living in God's grace, and so equally cannot say of anybody
that he has lost it. And so, as we must with absolutely certain confidence in God hope in God's merciful grace for
ourselves, we have the same duty of hope (since we must
love our neighbor as ourself) on behalf of each of our neigh-
bors. And we know that in every human being there is an
eternal destiny in the making, coming to maturity through
all the trivialities of everyday life and commonplace humanity.

We know all that. We have never disputed it. But we do
not live it. This infinite dignity, this indestructible nobility,
this fact, that every human being is infinitely more than a
human being, remains to a large extent a sort of thin Sunday-
ideology, something we do not dispute in theory because it
does us no harm and does not prevent us from sticking to
everyday norms and attitudes in the everyday world. But
suppose that our sober everyday eyes should look at this neighbor of ours and see through all his physical degeneracy,

through the screen of his instinctual life, his conditioning, his psychology in so far as it is physiologically determined. Suppose they should see even through all that this other person thinks about himself and desires for himself, through all his self-interpretation, which is never capable of saying the ultimate truth about a man; that they should see through all that fate has done in the course of such a life, in terms of heredity, upbringing, environment, latent sickness, psychopathology; and even through true and appalling guilt, since it too is not the ultimate thing, it too (as Paul says) is embraced and included within the greater and mightier mercy of God. Suppose that our eyes, seeing through all this, should seek and find that which is most real and ultimate in this other person: God, with his love and his mercy, who has conferred an eternal dignity upon this person and offers himself to him, without repentance, in the incomprehensible prodigality of the divine foolishness of love. Suppose that we should see in this way not at some solemn, ceremonial moment but at the point where this man confronts us with his blank gaze, his lack of receptivity, his reek of poverty; at the point where he rises up before us, sullen and resentful, malicious, unteachable, stupidly cunning. Supposing we could indeed see in this way, then we should really come to meet this man with a reverent humility, in which we would realize that we cannot recognize any higher dignity or holier calling in ourselves than that which is present in him.

And if we did look at him like this, in reverent humility, then we would see Christ in him: the incarnate Word of the Father, who is everywhere honored and adored (whether this is realized or not) whenever one human being is taken absolutely seriously by another; whenever a person recognizes that it is impossible to have any experience with a fellow human being, however evil and appalling, which would involve looking through him into emptiness instead of into the mystery of God, in whom is hidden the eternal image of this man, without which (as Angelus Silesius says) God "cannot for a moment live." Man, in his nature and his determination towards grace, exists because God has willed the God-Man: because *he* has willed *himself as man;* because henceforth there is no longer any truth of God which is not truth of man; because (this is so only out of free grace, but it really is so) God would not be, if man were not. And so, whenever the most wretched of human creatures, some mean, stupid scoundrel, is received reverently and humbly into our own hearts, it is Christ who is being received and discovered. And (may one dare to say it?) there best of all. For where have we a better hope of finding God than in such a case? When the spell of man's own greatness and beauty, his own goodness and splendor, is cast upon us, this may indeed act as a door into the infinite greatness, beauty, goodness and splendor of God. It may, in itself. But we are so apt in such a case to stop short at the human greatness as such. This is something we cannot do with poor sinners, when we discover what is abiding and indestructible in them, when we honor what they perhaps take no account of in themselves, when we believe in God in them, though they do not find him in themselves.

And there is still another sense of finding God in our humiliated neighbor. When we go to meet this wretched neighbor in the way that we should, when we care about him without any supporting feeling of instinctive, physiologically-conditioned sympathy, when we forgive even while feeling that we are being made fools of by doing so, when we really pour ourselves out without the reward of a feeling of satisfaction and without any return in gratitude, when our very encounter with our neighbor makes us unutterably lonely and all such love seems to be only an annihilating leap into an absolute void, then that is really God's hour in our life; that is when *he* is there. Assuming that we don't turn back; assuming that it doesn't get us down, that we don't find ourselves some sort of compensation elsewhere, that we don't complain, that we don't feel sorry for ourselves, that we keep quiet about it and really accept and commit ourselves to the absence of ground under our feet and the foolishness of such love. Then it is God's hour: then this seemingly sinister abyss in our existence, as it opens up in this hopeless experience of our neighbor, will be the abyss of God himself, communicating himself to us; it will be the beginning of the coming of his infinity, where all roads disappear, and which feels like nothingness because it is infinity.

When we have had such an encounter with our neighbor, an encounter in which we break through the instability of what is earthly in him and seem to fall into a void; when we have let go of ourselves in it and no longer belong to ourselves; when we have denied ourselves and no longer dispose of ourselves for purposes of power or self-enjoyment; when everything in such an encounter, and ourselves too, seems to have fallen away from us into infinite remoteness, then we begin to find God. Then this lonely, silent void of the interior man, who seems to have been as it were destroyed, begins to be filled with God; then we find God, we find Christ, who fell into the hands of the Father when, as he was dying, he recognized his God-forsakenness. At the beginning, this may seem alien to us; this loss of ourselves may terrify us, and the temptation may come upon us to flee in our terror back to intimacy and gratitude and the sense of being loved. Indeed, it will often be right and necessary for us to do so. But we should gradually learn to find life in this death, intimacy in this loneliness, God in this forsakenness. It is only when we can do this, when we can find and experience God himself in this disappointment of our love for our neighbor, that our love for our neighbor becomes mature, and an act of the Holy Spirit in us. It can then become really long-suffering and patient, without malice, never ceasing to hope, never disillusioned. It will always find God.

It is not to be thought that this means that our neighbor, especially when he is a disappointing neighbor, is simply a means by which we practice ascetical renunciation so as to create that void within us which God then freely and mercifully fills with the unutterable intimacy of his presence. For none of this happens unless we truly love the person in question, truly accepting him for what he is, and not making this love into a means to anything. But if, without aiming at it, this God-loving love of our neighbor does find God while seeking our neighbor, then this lonely experience of God, taking place within the death of all self-seeking, becomes a final possibility for us, a final source of strength for loving our neighbor "to the last." We really die of this love; to die without despair (and despair puts an end to love) can only be done if we die into the infinite life of God. So we must love and seek our neighbor, and not our own fulfillment and perfection, but this can only be done "to the last" if we find God in it and if this true love of our neighbor is embraced and redeemed, preserved and liberated, by happening within the love of God, as a finding of God in Christ. Anyone, then, who exposes himself to this death-dealing adventure of an unconditional love of his neighbor will find God; and whoever finds God can love his neighbor as himself. He will receive that clearness of vision which belongs to the faith which sees the reality of God even in the most abandoned of men, making him in all truth worthy of being loved with humble reverence.

We find Christ our Lord in the prisoners; we have got to find him there; he is really there to be found, and to be found in such a way that our encounter with him will also be for our salvation and our happiness.

Ourselves in the Prisoners

We find ourselves in the prisoners when we see in them the hidden truth of our own situation.

Every human being is continually running away from himself. Only those saints who have attained perfection could say that they no longer deceive themselves about themselves. Only the perfect have stopped repressing the truth of God within them. The truth that we are sinners; the truth that we are self-seekers; the truth that in a thousand different ways, crude or subtle, we are always trying to serve God *and* ourselves; the truth that we are cowardly, easygoing, lazy, refractory servants of God; the truth that we do not do what we ought to do: love God with our *whole* heart and *all* our strength. Together with the Scriptures and the teachings of the early Church, we can express the content of this repressed truth by acknowledging that we are unfree, prisoners, unless the Spirit of God, his grace, sets us free. We may be free in a bourgeois, legal sense: we may be responsible for our actions, not only in the sight of men but also in the sight of God and his most merciful and just judgment. But if we have not been set free by the Spirit of God into the freedom of Christ, then for all this earthly freedom and its corresponding responsibility in the sight of God, we are nevertheless helpless and hopeless prisoners in the prison of our guilt, our unsaved condition, our inability to perform any saving act.

And these people whom we visit are an image of this: an image of all those who sit in darkness and the shadow of death, imprisoned in the dungeon of their own finitude, the dungeon of a freedom which has not yet been set free by Christ and is still enslaved to sin, the flesh and the power of the evil one. The prison in which your work goes on is an image of this prison of the world, not in an external, artificial sense, through some artificial analogy, but an image in the sense of a manifestation, a true and real type, the making visible of a hidden reality which makes itself manifest and tangible in this real symbol. For no matter what may be the immediate causes of prisons and of the plight of their inmates, the one ultimate cause is the guilt of mankind from its beginnings onwards; the guilt which propagates itself through all individual personal guilt; the same guilt which confronts us incarnate in poverty, sickness and unhappiness; the guilt which is a power in our own lives too, so that what we call prisons and penitentiaries are, to a Christian understanding of things, simply individual cells of a perceptible kind in that one great prison which Scripture calls "the world," "this age," "the evil world," the domain of the Prince of this world, the realm of the powers of darkness, death and evil. When you go from your own surroundings into a prison, you do not go out of a world of harmony, light and order into a world of guilt and unfreedom: you stay where you have been all the time. It is merely made clearer to your bodily senses what has been surrounding you all the time: the unfreedom of guilt, the imprisonment from which Christ's grace alone can set us free into the freedom of the children of God.

But (it might be objected), true though all this is, we ourselves are nevertheless those who have been redeemed, who have been liberated into this freedom, we are no longer in servitude to sin, the law, vanity and death! So it is with us; we hope it is; each day we strengthen our hearts anew in this hope, which may often, alas, seem like a hope against hope. We comfort our hearts anew each day with this hope, which faith alone, and no experience or pharisaic self-consciousness of ours, can give us. But equally, so long as we are pursuing our pilgrimage in hope, not in vision, and are redeemed in hope, so long as we are still marching and not yet at the goal, we are still as it were prisoners, whose prison door is opening at this very moment, who are suddenly being bidden, by an unlooked-for miracle of grace, to get up and go, like Peter being struck on the side by the angel: "Get up quickly, dress yourself and follow me" (Acts 12, 7-8), while the chains fall from our hands. We are people who have entered into freedom and can be said to have attained it precisely in so far as we do not think of it as a possession that can be taken for granted; in so far as we are aware, in fear and trembling, of whence we come; in so far as we know that we can only receive this gift of the freedom of Christ with impunity, without its becoming our ultimate damnation, if we accept it simply and solely as our redemption from slavery by the grace of God.

And again: even if we are the redeemed; even if in those who are in Christ Jesus, those who believe in him and love him, there is no longer anything worthy of damnation; even if the ground of our being, its innermost center, is graced and filled with the holy Pneuma of God; even if, then, what is in us can no longer make us, as indivisible subjects before God's judgment, worthy of damnation, yet the heritage of the past is still at the same time ultimately and indissolubly still in us. Or is concupiscence not still to be found in us? Is there not in us that which is in the world, the lust of the eyes and the lust of the flesh and the pride of life? Are we not sick, compulsive, only too apt to deceive ourselves, egoists, slaves (if only in an attenuated form) to our cravings for this and that? Supposing someone came to us—supposing *God* came to us, and lit up the interior of our hearts not merely with the cold inexorability of a psychotherapist but with the incorruptibility of the ultimate truth of the Thrice-Holy One; supposing he were to analyze our motives, our attitudes, our behavior-patterns, our secret impulses, hidden even from ourselves; if he were to confront us with ourselves, stripped and naked, as we are, not as we like to appear to ourselves, should we not then have to fall down in terror before this judge of our hearts, crying "Depart from me, for I am a sinful man, O Lord"? Would not his grace, by which we are made holy, then appear to us as something which we simply are not; would we not have to say, brokenly and with tears, "That is You, that is Your inconceivable love, the unreasonable prodigality, so to say, of Your mercy; but I am not that; I am dull and cowardly and shut up within myself; I am a confused and tangled bundle of impulses and chances and external determinisms of which it is never possible to know at any moment what is genuinely my own, what is mere façade, what is real, whether shabbiness is the humility of the virtue that is in me or virtue is the disguise for the wretchedness in me"? Should we not have to pray with tears, "If thou, O Lord, shouldst mark iniquities, Lord, who shall endure it? Enter not into judgment with me, cleanse me from my secret sin!"

Should we not then have to recognize and acknowledge that we are not so essentially different from those poor sinners whom we visit in the prisons? Should we not have to say that what distinguishes us from them is merely the fact that the *fomes peccati*, which is in us in the same way as it is in them, has not—because of circumstances which are no merit of ours but matters of situation, fate and chance—brought us into conflict, as it has them, with the external order of men and society? We can indeed be grateful to God for these very circumstances: even extremely so. But does that differentiate us so much from them that, because we are the redeemed, we can no longer see ourselves in them, and must deny that our own image, stripped of its masks, looks out at us from them? The more so as we can never say that they are not in the grace of God, since everything that confronts us in them is just as liable to be sickness as guilt, or to be the guilt of society, in which we too may perhaps have our part, having drawn on it, and continuing to draw on it, for our revenue of comfort and bourgeois security and affluence. And the more so again, since we are not certain that we are in God's grace.

So, then, we meet ourselves when we meet prisoners in prison. They present our own image to us, that image which we must face continually, day after day, if we hope to find the grace of God for ourselves; for that grace is only given to those who acknowledge themselves as sinners and build their lives on one thing only, the incomprehensible grace of God who takes pity on the lost. We have no choice: either we are going to go through the prisons like pharisees, saying "Lord, I thank thee that I am not as one of these, robbers, swindlers, adulterers," or like the publican in Luke's gospel. He stood afar off, just as our unredeemed feelings find the prisons far off from God, beating his own breast and not someone else's (a thing we are apt to do when visiting in prison), and said, "God, be merciful to me a sinner!" (Luke 18, 9-14). Only if our attitude in the prisons is that of the publican in the Temple will the prison become for us poor sinners a temple from which we can return justified to our own homes. Otherwise we shall be going into the true prison of our own blindness, hypocrisy and pride, against which God sets his face, while those inside, perhaps, may be the ones who are justified and free in God's sight.

So, then, we find ourselves in the prisoners, seeing in them the hidden truth of our own situation.

In every life, and even in the holiest office a man can hold, there is one deadly enemy: habit and routine. Oh, we need habit and routine. We cannot live for long without them. They make many things easier for us which would otherwise soon be too much for our powers; they may often be a mild narcotic which God has mercifully supplied against the pain of living. But they are also the deadly enemy of our life and of the holy office we hold. They blunt us, they keep us going long after the real substance—spirit and love—has faded out of our work. And thus they may give us a "good conscience" when what we ought to have is a bad one. They make us take credit for our good deeds instead of beating our breasts because there is in them so little love, so little heart, so little humility and reverence for men, even those who are outcasts from society. We must keep fighting this deadly thing, habit, as though it were a cunning and mortally dangerous enemy.

This applies to your job, too. It is a grace from God to have his providence sustaining you in this battle, not only through the grace of that holy joy you feel as pastors over someone whom you have been able to bring back to the love of God, but also through all the sharp disappointments and bitterness of the job, all its failures, all the indifference which it meets, all that it can do to torment you and wear you down. If these experiences, those hard and bitter ones, force you out of the mediocrity of habit and routine, confront you with the question of what you really are trying to do in a job like this, and compel you to think about the real meaning and grace of such a calling, then this too is God's grace. And—again through the gentle and unobtrusive workings of grace in you—you should come to meet this grace, thinking and praying in the sight of God about what you are and what you are aiming at in this calling. And if, in the course of such a meditation, you also perhaps consider that, in the prisoners entrusted to our priestly care, we can truly and indeed find Christ for ourselves, and that, by encountering in them the reflection and likeness of our own situation, we may be re-called to that humility to which alone God's grace is promised, then such a meditation may well build up to greater fullness and completeness that unity between your calling and your life, your office and your own personal existence, which is, in the nature of things, made possible to an unsurpassed degree of splendor and grace in the calling of a priest.

5

The Parish Bookshop:
On the Theology of Books

If I am to say anything here to which one could (somewhat ambitiously) attach the title "On the Pastoral Theology of Books," I must begin by emphasizing the obvious: that there can be no question of so exalting the pastoral significance of books that by the end of it books would appear as about the most important means that can be used in pastoral work. It cannot be like that. This cannot be the object of a theological consideration of the work that you do. It always has to be stressed, in pastoral matters, that there is no one single all-purpose means for the building up of God's kingdom in the individual and in the Church. Everyone engaged in pastoral work is required to cultivate an attitude about this that is by no means easy to achieve: to carry out his own task and mission with as much devotion as though they were the only, or the most important, ones in the Church, and at the same time to be so modest in his thinking about them that he ungrudgingly gives everything else in the Church and her pastoral work the place due to it. But with this reservation, much can be said from a theological point of view of the meaning and significance of books and of working with them for the salvation of men.

When a theologian hears the word "book" and is expected to say something about it, he instinctively tries to take for his starting-point the Holy Book, Holy Scripture. This does indeed provide us with an approach to the matter, though not the only theologically conceivable one. The Church has a holy book, of which she says that God is its originator; that, inspired by the Holy Ghost, it contains without error the revelation of God for the salvation of men. She sees this book, furthermore, as a book which cannot be followed by anything of the same kind, a final and irreplaceable book for all time to come. She sees this book as the book out of which she lives, on which she draws for her preaching, and which is and always will be the norm for the content of her teaching and the guideline for her dogmatic decisions. Let us reflect a little on these dogmatic statements about the holy book.

In the first instance, such reflection should give us something like a shock: that a book should be so important that God himself makes himself its originator in a special and unique sense, and that it should be one of the essential, permanent, not-to-be-superseded constitutive elements of the Church. That such an origin and such significance for salvation should be attributed to a *book!* To something which did not even exist for the greater part of human history: yet mankind comes forth from God as its originator, and has in all ages been required to work out its supernatural salvation. For hundreds of thousands of years a history was going on which was not only human history but really salvation history, just as it is for us now; and there were no books. Now, suddenly, in the brief space of time (compared with the age of mankind) from Moses to our own day, a book is to be numbered amongst the things appointed by God as necessary for salvation, and to be placed alongside the sacrament on the Church's table.

Books have indeed made their entry into the innermost realm of the holy and the salvific. Should we say that in fact they came into existence *within* this religious sphere, with man, as *homo religiosus*, beginning to write and to put his writings into permanent, time-defying form basically because of his desire to embody the one abidingly valid word of revelation and the demands of tradition, so that the secular book is an offspring of the sacred book? Or should we say that books, secular in origin, have been consecrated and have entered into the realm of the holy? However that may be, books are something belonging to the most intimate sphere of man's being, the point where the encounter takes place between God and man through which come salvation and God's self-revelation. But this is something which has become the case only "recently," only since God, in the course of the immeasurably long history of his saving activity from paradise onwards, shed his anonymity and began a public and to some extent official salvation history with the Sinaitic covenant. But fundamentally this beginning is only a final preparation, the shadow cast before it of that real, personal entry of God into history, by which God becomes present in person within space and time, revealed in his most intimate life, finally established in the decision of his mercy, and communicated to man in his innermost glory.

Within this one saving event of the incarnation of the Word of God himself, books too make their appearance within salvation history. The consecration of books is an element in the incarnation of the Word of God. Because and in so far as God assumed human reality, making it his own reality by which he is revealed and communicated, to that extent too books are assumed and consecrated as an element in the existence of man as God wills him to be so as to be able to make a real encounter with the incarnate Word of God. As those hundreds of thousands of years of human history show, it is possible to be human without books. But it is possible to encounter the incarnate Word of God, in the way in which God willed, only in a community amongst whose constitutive elements is the Holy Book, as a medium in which that community possesses the abiding presence of Christ.

There is no sense in considering at length whether it would have been possible, in itself, for this drawing together of mankind and God to that point of convergence which we call Christ to have happened without the emergence, in and with the Church, of a Holy Book as something by which the Church is constituted, and as a means willed by God for making that eschatological point of convergence permanently present as long as this age of the world continues. Whatever may have been possible in the abstract, God did as a matter of concrete reality will that his absolute and abiding presence with mankind should be bound up with the emergence of a Holy Book. Now, the whole of world history has been willed and directed by God, without prejudice to its natural character, indeed precisely *in* its natural character, because and in so far as it was his will to give himself utterly, to give the intimate reality of himself, by the grace of the hypostatic union, to that which is not divine.

Since, then, natural realities are truly christocentric, and their natural character is not thereby encroached upon but in fact established, we must say that God willed that human history should come to the point of producing books because and in so far as he willed the Holy Book as a concrete element in the incarnation of his own Word. And hence, ultimately, springs all the dignity and significance of books. When we say, for instance, that the Church cannot cease to exist, so long as the doings and sufferings of history continue in this world; when we make this historical prognosis of faith, despite our experience of the transitoriness of all earthly things and of the endlessness of change, then we are also saying that books, that odd invention of recent times, are always going to remain, will never cease to be, will be part of mankind's existential reality until the last day. Thus books have entered into the sphere of the incarnate Word of God, of sacramentally mediated salvation and of eschatological finality; they are amongst the Church's necessary means for self-understanding.

The handing on of this Holy Book, the reading of it, the dissemination of it, the explanation and defense of it are thus really, *iure divino*, part of the essence of the Church and of Christian salvation. Thus in the dimension of the Church and her pastoral work, activity in respect of *one* book, at least, is something as indispensable, essential, irreplaceable and irremovable as, for instance, the primacy of the pope, the decisions of the teaching authority, preaching, and the administration of the sacraments. We have no need to make comparisons of the relative value of these individual essential constituents of salvation, of the Church, and of her pastoral activity. They may differ in value, just as the individual sacraments, without prejudice to their sacramentality, do not have the same value and ontological and existential density and power. This makes no difference to the fact that, along with all these other things, the Holy Book is, by the will of God, an irreducible constituent of the incarnational presence of the Word of God in the

Church for our salvation. Even though there may be a greater or lesser degree of directness and vitality in the relationship of the individual Christian to this book, if only because there are, and it is right that there should be, illiterates in the Church, yet the Church *as a whole* has an essential and absolutely necessary relationship to this book.

This is the ground of the dignity and significance in the Church of books in general and the service of books. In our christocentric theology of history, we see books, as a secular phenomenon, as having arisen in order to make possible and to lead up to the Holy Book. And if this is true, unrealistic as it may sound, then all the more is it true that other books *post Christum natum et post sacram Scripturam scriptam*, at least in so far as they come into existence within the sphere of the Church, are a sequel, an echo, an interpretation and explanation of that book. All "religious writing" is essentially a service of that book, and hence participates in its way and to its degree in the dignity, the indispensability and the permanent validity of Sacred Scripture in the Church.

This other writing is not inspired and does not need to be; it can be left by God to the incalculable and never wholly assessable processes of history, to a degree that is essentially not possible in the case of those writings which are part of what constitutes the primitive Church as a permanent initial stage determining the Church's entire future; and which are therefore required to have an absolute "purity," so that they can be *norma non normata* to be applied to all later preaching and writing by the Church's teaching and pastoral office, exercising its gift of discernment under the guidance of the Spirit. But in a Catholic understanding of Scripture there will be a greater and perhaps more down-to-earth stress than in a Protestant one on the necessity of interpretation and continual, fresh actualization of the Scriptures in the Church. Whatever may be the truth about the sufficiency of Scripture, however much one may agree that tradition, while always necessary as the interpreter of Scripture, being the Church's here-and-now proclamation of the faith, does not actually supply any material content independent of and additional to Scripture, nevertheless for a Catholic understanding this here-and-now interpretation, this dogmatic unfolding of Scripture, is in any case so necessary to it, and to its permanent significance in the Church that, for instance, such interpretation is not only "theologizing" about the written word of God but can be a definitively valid utterance making an absolute claim on faith.

But if in the concrete life of the Church of the Holy Book there is this essential and necessary interpretation of that Book, then there must necessarily also be *written* interpretation in books. Hence it is not surprising that in the concrete the concept of tradition as a criterion of true belief alway implies in practice having recourse to the *books* of the Fathers and theologians: recourse to books as interpretations of the Holy Book. The continual fresh production of new books thus belongs to the essence of the Church's history, precisely because it is her task to serve the continual here-and-now reality of the one Book; precisely because all these many books have got to lead back to that one Book.

This very return to the sources is only possible through the continual fresh production of new books. If truth has a history, and above all that truth which has been revealed in salvation history in an historical process and is to be transmitted as such in time, then this history, ever since there has been a

Holy Book, must necessarily also be a history of books. The sigh of the Preacher (Eccles. 12, 12) may indeed ring true today, that of making many books there is no end; there may be far too much poor and mediocre stuff being written in the Church; it may be necessary, in the sense of a necessity of salvation history, to say of the writing of books in the Church what has to be said of the servant-image of the Church and her sinfulness and wretchedness in general; but it still remains true that to the life of the Church, to her essential self-fulfillment in the concrete, to her history, to the carrying out of her task and mission for the salvation of the world, belong not only the one Holy Book but also all the books which somehow, though perhaps in a remote and indirect way, serve that Book.

And the work of your Borromeo Society is essentially part of the service of that Book. This work with books for the Book, which is of the essence of the Church, can of course be carried out in many different forms and ways: including other ways, obviously, than those done by you. But it is as with the preaching of the word: in any particular concrete sermon a particular preacher chooses particular words, and the preacher, the sermon and the words could all be different; yet when all this happens, it is really the word of God which is spoken. In the same way, though your work and service obviously do not, as concrete facts, belong necessarily to the realization of the Church's nature, yet when they *are* done, they are truly a realization of that aspect of her essential nature which, through the service of books, makes God's Book permanently present to every age. Hence all the value and necessity of your work. If it is true that God's word in God's Book has, by his will, made itself the permanent prerequisite for his sheer presence in the Church, then this can also be said analogically of books in the Church. This means that preaching, as the proclamation of the word of God in the concrete here-and-now of the Church and of the individual human being, can and must also be given concrete shape in the books that are written in the Church. From the theological point of view, books have essentially the same function for the Church and the Christian as the oral proclamation of the word. This is why the Church's law requires a book to have, if we may so express it, a *missio canonica* and a sort of apostolic succession. The Church's imprimatur for a book is not so much a sort of police supervision of public opinion in the Church as a positive authorization (though an extremely nuanced one) of this word for the Church.

It may well be true, and indeed of great importance for a sound theology of preaching, that the spoken word, precisely *as* spoken, has an irreplaceable function, similar to the spoken word in the sacraments, for which written communication will not do. But this indisputable "plus" of the spoken word comes from its interpersonal function in the Church as a holy community; it arises, if we may put it this way, from the essentially liturgical function of the word which is immediately addressed, in the first instance, to the community as a whole, so that the community is given its here-and-now corporeal reality by the common hearing of the word. You, who do not publish or distribute liturgical books for public worship, are in the service of books intended for the individual, solitary reader, not immediately for reading aloud to the community, not part of that proclamation which constitutes the community, not having the liturgical character of the spoken word in the Church. But this does not mean that they are incapable of being a here-and-now communication of the word of God and hence of participating in the dignity of the spoken word of God as it is preached. For, while the individual human being is indeed a member of the Church as the community, established in salvation history and founded in the Holy Pneuma, of those who are redeemed in faith and love, yet the individual human being is not wholly absorbed into his strictly community function as a member. Not even in the Church. The saving word of God is also addressed to him as an individual: who never indeed ceases to be a member of the Church, but does not only stand before God, encountering the word of God, at those times when he is actually operating his membership of the Church within the structure of the community.

The word of God wills to encounter the individual in the unique and irreplaceable singularity and solitariness of his own heart and conscience. It does not thereby cease to be that word of God whose mediating tangibility and historicity are to be found in Sacred Scripture. And hence books of explanation and meditation read privately can indeed also be the event of the hearing of the word of God, so that these books too, like preaching, participate in the dignity of the corporeal character of the word of God. Hence service of these books is essentially service of the word of God, and participates in the necessity, the saving significance, the dignity, the divine and apostolic mission of this "service of the word" (Acts 6, 8).

There is another angle altogether from which it is possible to approach the theological meaning of books and of your work: that of a theological anthropology. Man is placed in an ineradicable dualism of two basic lines of self-fulfillment: he is a being who is thrust out of himself into the world and the human community, and he is a being who turns back upon himself. This double bent, to take possession of himself and of what is not himself, in knowledge and love, constitutes his essential nature. The going out of himself and entering into himself condition each other. If he did not go out into the world, to the Other as "thou" and (so far as one can still call this a going out) to God, he would find nothing on entering into himself but the hellish emptiness and empty isolation of the damned. And if he only went out of himself, then he would indeed be alienated from himself, lost, scattered piecemeal. Gathering and scattering, entry into oneself and going out of oneself, belong to each other essentially. And what constitutes a true human being and Christian is that he entrusts himself freely to both these basic movements, as both under the direction of one same God, and, serene in this creaturely confidence, refrains from making either of them an absolute.

But this ineradicable dualism of entry into oneself and going out of oneself must necessarily, in a creature which belongs to time, without prejudice to the essential ordering of these two movements towards each other, work itself out in a temporal rhythm. While it is true that we have each of them only in the other, we must yet strive by turns now for one of them and now for the other, steering towards one of them without forgetting the other, tranquilly ready for the other one even while we are striving after this one. To have the courage and freedom to live in time as a creature of time —to be a pilgrim passing through a series of different realizations of what he is meant to be—is part of the very nature of a Christian and of his confidence in the rightness of the plural order of being, in which each moment and element makes its demands and imposes its obligations and at the same time sends one on to the next thing, leaving one free for it.

So there is a turning inwards and a turning outwards in human life, basic themes of man's existence the realization of which must necessarily be successive. There are solitude and society, silence and speech, gathering and scattering, inhaling and exhaling, listening and talking, sitting still and moving about. It is hence of crucial importance for man and his salvation that he should not make an absolute of either of these basic themes of his existence; that he should be genuinely and concretely convinced that he can never entirely eliminate even their temporal alternation from his temporal life; that in fact he can never have everything at once and all in one. But in the present context this means that man has got to have a time for leisure, for silence, for turning back on himself, for gathering himself together and entering into himself, and that nothing else will do instead.

The style of this turning inwards, the way it is done in the concrete, may change very much in the course of the different ages of man's history. There will always be the danger that people, including Christians, will produce reactionary criticisms of new, emergent styles in the fulfillment of elements in human existence, failing to realize that even the most important and non-expendable of basic human realities can be preserved and put into practice in different ways from those followed hitherto. For instance, the fact that authority, reverence for parents, differentiation between generations, etc., are permanent structures in any genuine, healthy humanity does not by any means imply, nor does the legitimate defense of them require, that they should have to be embodied in the historically conditioned forms of the eighteenth century. The same certainly holds true of human leisure and withdrawal into oneself. It may in many cases have to be achieved and cultivated today in different ways from those of former times. Seldom will a man of today be found sitting in his "arbor." But the real thing involved in this can only be lost if man himself is lost; it has got to be constantly reacquired and given whatever concrete form is being offered to us for it today; it has got to be constantly defended by a genuine, responsible ascesis against the dangers which constantly threaten it.

If man is thus to withdraw into himself without being frightened of silence and solitude, without giving way to the panic of a gregarious animal separated from the herd, then this movement of return cannot simply mean the production of a state of absolute emptiness. It may be that something of that sort exists as well. The experience of overpowering, limitless emptiness, the disappearance of all formulas and outlines so as to make room for the forbidding presence of the nameless mystery, may also be one of man's indispensable experiences, without which he can never become so aware of God as he is called upon and required to be. But this is not in the majority of cases the meaning of solitary leisure. In a mysterious way, the return into oneself, while representing a particular phase in the rhythm of existence, takes along with it the world towards which one was turned outwards before. If a man did not do this he would not be able to arrive at that self-discovery which is the goal of his turning in upon himself. Even in this solitude, he needs to place himself over against something other than himself if he is to come to himself: he needs a point of leverage outside himself

in order to be able to move his own subjective world. But he
needs to be able to set this world of his over against himself;
it has got to be not too overpowering for him, but to be present
in a muted form, so to speak; it needs to be reduced and con-
densed to its essentials so that it will not overwhelm him but
that he, in mastering it, will be able to find himself and discover what is his own as distinct from all else.

What provides this concentrated, muted, manageable presence of the world in the solitude in which man enters into himself is books. Primarily, of course, books which are an
imaginative presentation of human reality and man's world.
When we speak here of books and the significance they have
for man's withdrawal into solitude, we do not of course
mean books whose perusal is simply a handling of the so-
called "real" external world: technical books in the widest
sense, which are basically just an extended treatment of directions for using the external world. What we mean is the
kind of book by which the real content of man's world is concentrated and made transparent, and which thus addresses
itself to that in man which is genuinely humane. We mean
books which can be called humane (and thus of course truly
Christian). We mean the kind of books which make it possible or easier for a man who has entered into his own solitude
to remember and interiorize that world in which, for the rest
of the time, he is exposed to action and suffering; which
present man's world to him with precisely that degree of
nearness and detachment needed to enable him to discover
himself and his true relationship to the world.

These are the books for which you work; the books on the
shelves under your care belong not to technology but to the
humanities. To get a still better grasp of the dignity and

urgency of this work, two things should be considered. The world which these books are meant to make available and manageable to man in his musings is clearly in the first instance simply man's world: that is, a world which is indeed humane, spiritual, with mysterious depths, perhaps even numinous, but not primarily the religious world strictly as such, but the secular world; the world of the mind, of human destiny, of joy and death, love and solitude, work and merry meetings, of heroes and of disaster, of nature and history in so far as these are essentially powers of man's existence. The religious and Christian and ecclesiastical elements are not excluded from all this and are not to be denied, because these are or can be genuine forces in life as it is lived and suffered. But books for leisure, books which are a means to man's self-recollection and entry into himself through imaginatively bringing the world to him and setting it apart from him, these are primarily secular books in the sense indicated, not religious books in the strictest sense. A religious entry into oneself in the strictest sense of the word does indeed exist too, when man, summoned by the word of God reaching him through history, consciously and explicitly addresses himself to the question of his salvation, putting himself in the presence of the mystery of his existence and explicitly calling that mystery by the name of God. But that turning inwards of which we have been speaking here, as a basic act of human existence finding its expression in rhythmic alternation in time, is to be understood in a wider sense, though it is true that all such turning inwards is in some fashion a prelude and beginning to that ultimate self-discovery which can only be made in the presence of God. Thus it holds good that the means to this entry into oneself is primarily the book that is humane rather than explicitly religious. But yet it has to be seen and explicitly grasped that this very entry into oneself, and precisely this kind of book, do, in their very secularity, have a religious significance.

In Catholic teaching and theology there is an essential distinction between nature and grace, culture and Church, secular history and salvation history. But what this distinction does not imply is that what is natural and secular has no significance for what is religious. Not that the significance of the secular and humane can be or ought to be reckoned simply in terms of its being an instrumental means, of being something *useful* to the religious sphere. Whenever the secular, the "merely" human, is seen narrowly and clericalistically only in terms of its usefulness to religion in the narrower sense or, more narrowly still, to the ecclesiastical sphere, it withers away and loses, in the long run, the very significance that it does have for religion in the narrower sense. But the genuinely secular, the humane in its uninhibited, immediate manifestation, has fundamental religious significance. If a man wanted to be *only a homo religiosus*, living exclusively and directly on his explicitly Christian impulses, he would become humanly impoverished and cease, as a spiritual subject, to have within himself the resources needed for a complete development of his very Christianity. There is indeed, depending on the particular calling made to each individual, the possibility of an ascetical renunciation of fulfillment within this world as an act of faith in the reality of grace, which cannot be controlled from this world; and this attitude needs to exist in some measure in the Church and in some way in each individual Christian life.

But if anyone thinks that absolute flight from the world,

so far as is physically possible, is the one true way in which his religious life can grow in its complete realization, then it is not a Christian ideal that he is proclaiming; possibly a Buddhist one. A going out into the non-religious world, a direct relationship with the world not primarily directed and mediated by Christianity, is, however paradoxical it may sound, amongst the necessary bases of a sound religious life in general and, to a heightened degree, of the life of the lay Christian in particular. A Christian must work out his Christianity in the material of the world. But he can do this only if he has familiarized himself with this material. And such familiarity is possible only if he really throws himself into the world, wholeheartedly and without reservations, trusting in the one God of heaven *and earth*. The secular world, as secular, has an inner mysterious depth, in all its earthly mysteries from birth to death, through which, by the grace of God, it is open to God and his infinitely incomprehensible love even when it is not, before receiving the explicit message of the gospel, aware of it. Not only are there many anonymous Christians; there is also an anonymously Christian world. For whenever its demands and its reality are really met and endured in the whole breadth and depth of natural human existence and in the totality of a human life, then, according to Christian teaching, the grace of Christ is already at work and this response and endurance are already something Christian, though they may be explicitly only secular and natural.

Hence, anything that mediates to men a genuinely humane understanding of life and the world is mediating the indispensable prerequisites of Christianity. In such a situation, grace is fashioning its own natural foundations. Indeed, what is inexplicitly present is often more than mere nature: it is the healing action of the God of grace and eternal life, protecting and saving this natural value. Hence it is not the case that working for secular and humane books cannot be a religious task, part of the mission of the Church. It is not the case that such work would take on Christian and missionary significance only when explicitly and intentionally linked with religion, in a means-to-end relationship, like a Western shown in the parish hall for altar boys only.

A directly appreciable synthesis of the humane and the religious, in that kind of interpenetration which was possible in the Middle Ages and still, to a large extent, in the Baroque period, is today largely impossible. Not because the world has become evil and godless but simply because—ultimately by God's will and his guidance of history—the natural world, which is also God's world and his creation, has attained to such a degree of explicitness, articulateness and development of its potentialities that an ubiquitous presence of directly explicit and perceptible Christianity is simply not possible any more, nor even desirable. There never has been a time when every single thing really was explicitly Christian, still less ecclesiastical, in its form and structure. What was explicitly merely secular has always existed. And if today it exists more explicitly, in a more developed form, in almost overwhelming variety and magnificence, and not only in the realm of technology, economics and politics but also that of science, art, literature and cultural values in general; if today aesthetic values, artistic production and the humanities in general no longer find the material for their fulfillment merely in the religious sphere, but independently of religion as well; then this is not, fundamentally and as a whole, something which

Christians should grieve over, mourning for a medieval ideal, still less try to put into reverse, but something which was meant to happen by the will of God and will go on happening. This secularity in the cultural dimension, willed by God, does of course bring with it the danger of an unchristian secularization of the *whole* of human existence; and it may in a certain sense make it harder for people to avoid forgetting God amidst the splendor of the world. But a real Christian has the duty and the right to accept his situation in the modern world uninhibitedly, as one in which it is basically as possible to be a good Christian as it was when writers and scientists were under clerical direction, literature was almost coterminous with religious literature, and if a painter wanted to paint a human act he had to represent St. Laurence.

What all this means is that we can and must uninhibitedly take account of the fact that there is, and ought to be, a humane literature which is neither explicitly religious nor a pedagogical means to a religious end, but which does have religious significance. And to be in the service of such literature, which is a protection and development of man precisely as man, is of real Christian and religious significance in an age when the greatest threat to religion is perhaps precisely in its *human* dimension. Perhaps this literature cannot be called "Christian" in the explicit sense; but that does not by any means make it anti-Christian or even a-Christian. There are paintings which, while not suitable for hanging in a church, because they do not have explicitly Christian themes or could not count on being received with general understanding by the congregation, are nevertheless much more "Christian" in their human substance (given its concrete expression, perhaps, simply in still-life objects or a human face) than some painting lacking in human substance but supposed to represent St. Joseph. Similarly, a literature whose immediate themes are pre-religious may, in what it says and the way it says it, be so truly a *praeparatio Evangelii* that it is better deserving of the name of "Christian" literature than one that takes religion for its theme in a way which fails to achieve full human realization. So to work for books of this sort is not merely a necessary concession to a public with little interest in religion; not the harmless pedagogical trick of supplying three secular books so as to be able to include one religious one; it is in itself a thoroughly Christian mission and task, and does not cease to be so because other people, non-Christians, are seriously carrying out the same service. The days will certainly not come again when, as was still the case in the eighteenth century, 90% of books published were theological, whereas in Western Germany in 1955 the proportion was 6.2%. If those days did come again, all it would mean would be that the majority of people were illiterate and reading nothing at all, so that religious books as such would not really have grown to any greater importance than they have today.

For books of the kind you deal with are really a product of the nineteenth century. Books in the sense of a fairly long, connected treatment of some matter in writing, aimed in principle at a wide audience, had existed for long before that: books multiplied by copying for at least some thousands of years, printed books since Gutenberg, that is, the middle of the fifteenth century. But the books to which you devote your efforts represent something essentially more than a mere quantitative intensification of the circulation increase brought in by printing. For up to the nineteenth century, books were a privilege of a particular cultural and social stratum, the "educated"; they served the intellectual needs of a small, comprehensible group. Today everyone can read; modern techniques make possible the production of really large editions; books are aimed at the unknown reader, at everyman: they are no longer one of the distinguishing characteristics of particular social groups but are part of everybody's life, even if it remains a fact that in West Germany today 35% of the population do not possess a book. Books have become a mass product of the masses. The dangers in this phenomenon may well be truly pointed out: books have become subject to the laws of the market like any other product; they have become dependent on an irrelevant principle, the incalculable whims and caprice of an anonymous public, an amorphous entity which determines what shall and shall not be printed. We may speak, with truth, of the book industry, and all the damage and dangers implied in the word. But unless we are in favor of illiteracy, we cannot be against the facts bound up with the nature of the modern book; there is nothing for it but to see the dangers inherent in these facts, avoid them and combat them, and for the rest humbly and confidently recognize the chance God is offering in these facts. And the modern book does also offer this holy opportunity for good: many can be addressed both by the humane and the divine word; to many the true depth and splendor of the human and divine world can be mediated and made present by the printed word—many who otherwise, in the speechless desert of dreary everyday life, would experience little of true reality, despite all their so-called "experience of life," for what is genuine and holy, eternal and valid, whether of man or of God, can only be found in everyday life when

our eyes and our hearts have been opened to it in hours
that lie outside everyday life.

The accessibility of the masses through books implies too
an accessibility through books of numerous individuals in their
true personal uniqueness. In Germany in 1956 at least 13,000
different books were published (taking a minimum of forty-
nine pages as constituting a "book"), of which (these are the
1955 figures) 20% were "belles lettres," 6.2% religion and
theology, 6.3% history (and only, for instance, 5% science
and mathematics, 4% technology). In face of this it is not
possible to say that books have no future in the age of radio,
television, films and illustrated periodicals. Of course the
size of the edition of any book may well seem minute beside the millions-a-week mass circulation of the periodicals.
But all that has happened here is that technology has given
expression to something that was there in any case: the fact
that in the course of their lives people say a great many
superficial, commonplace, quickly forgotten words, and very
few with any eternal content. It was formerly the case (ap-
proximately, of course) that men could afford to print only
such words as had some divine and human weight; today it is
economically possible to print cheap talk as well as speak it.
But this does not make much real difference. It will still be
the few words with eternity in them that go on being real
in face of the many words of commonplace talk; the books
that belong to our hours of silence will remain, though the
illustrated periodicals may lie all over the place, the radio
blare at us from every side, and the cinemas be filled to
overflowing. Why should we abandon the struggle and the
hope of making the civilization of the masses the means of
achieving a culture for the many? If a person gives up this

struggle, with its hope-against-hope, all he proves is that he himself is only capable of being an atom in the mass. Your work is a share in this struggle. You work with books that, being humane, carry out a religious task, even when they are only humane, and with religious books as such. You try to convey them to the largest possible number of individuals, so that they will be able to take something of the genuine and humane world, and some word of God's message, with them into that quiet solitude in which an individual first begins to become a true human being: one who has come to himself, who freely accepts himself and his whole life, and who really becomes responsible to himself by speaking that word of love which is his response to God and to all things.

6

The Theological Meaning of Devotion to the Heart of Jesus

A dogmatic theologian finding himself called on nowadays to talk about devotion to the Heart of Jesus could in a sense take an easy way out by simply referring to Pius XII's great encyclical *Haurietis aquas* of May 15, 1956. Here, going beyond all that was given by Leo XIII and Pius XI, we do indeed have a comprehensive treatise on everything connected with this devotion. But this can equally well work the other way: since it is almost impossible to add anything to this treatise by the Church's supreme teacher, and since that teaching, in the actual terms there expressed, is bound to be repeatedly studied from now on, it is legitimate to produce a few pages intended neither as a summary of nor an addition to that teaching, but which, without aiming so high, merely offer a few very subjective marginal observations on this theme.

Man is not God, but exists in relation to God. Hence on the one hand he cannot, either in his being or in his thought and love, be and possess everything in one act (for then he would be God); but neither can he do without a unity, repeatedly sought after and achieved, within the necessary multiplicity of his being and his spiritual activity (for then he would not be a spiritual being existing in relation to the one

God). Hence, in his religion as in everything else, he must necessarily keep going out into the multiplicity of things as they are: many articles in his creed, many forms of his liturgy, many patterns and objects for his various religious acts; he has to love both God and man, go out of himself into a multiplicity of good works, and yet, as a contemplative person, enter into the innermost center of his grace-endowed being, where God and he are alone. So long as he is a pilgrim not yet with God, there will be this pluralism of a going out into inescapable multiplicity and a search for a unity embracing all the components of his temporal historical existence (which is what makes it possible for him to do, successively, these many different things), all that gives rise to the varied and eventful adventure of his mental and spiritual life and at the same time to the pain, never assuaged, of never being really able to possess all in one and one in all. This simple truth, which nevertheless dominates all the dimensions of a human being, needs to be kept in mind when trying to grasp the significance and the limitations of devotion to the Heart of Jesus.

Jesus Christ is the mediator; he is the unity in which God, who is all in one in simplicity, has taken to himself the multiplicity of things and their "thirst for unity"; for he has taken creatureliness (which is never one-in-all), and moreover intellectual creatureliness (with its longing for unity) to himself as his own reality, which is to remain so for ever (in its very multiplicity), and yet, while thus established in its permanent multiplicity, has been redeemed into the unity of God, unseparated from it (though also unmixed with it). Because *he* exists (the incarnate Word of the Father, in whom the Father totally utters himself without separation), unity does not automatically exclude the creature as something meaningless, and multiplicity is not simply something to be escaped from; God himself has entered into the creaturely diaspora; so there is no need, for those who do not want to leave it, to lose him, so long as we accept this dispersion and multiplicity as what it really is, something which has been truly made one (but not made uniform) in God's incarnate Word. So we can have our all-in-one, so far as it is appropriate to a creature to have it, only if we possess him who is both: all (the many) and one (the divine). If devotion to the Heart of Jesus is meant to be the ultimate, adoring invocation of the one, all-embracing ground of reality, and of the unity in the multiplicity of our religious life, then anyone who has found Jesus Christ is already in this sense an adorer of his Heart. Even if he does not know it, even if he does not mention the word "heart." Only if this is realized is it seriously possible to resolve the dilemma that either the people of earlier centuries were not good Christians (because they did not, explicitly, adore the Heart of Christ), or else this devotion cannot be something essentially Christian (because it did not always exist).

Now, this relationship to Jesus Christ is itself subject to historical change. It develops; it becomes differentiated and articulated; it has its own irreversible history (though a perpetual return to its origins and sources is also part of its essential character). Thus this relationship to Jesus Christ as the unifying center is itself subject to the law of inescapable plurality: we call him by many names and praise him in many tongues; he grows in our minds and hearts (and in the Church's mind and heart) through the centuries, and must so grow. And as he grows, he in his turn inevitably becomes—for the Church, its devotion, its theology—a world of realities and truths which it is beyond the mind of man to measure or hold together in his thought. After which, for a human being who aims to conform himself in simplicity and humility to his own plural and historical existence, there is nothing for it but to seek out once more some word of unity which he can invoke for the sake of his mind, his heart, his whole Christian existence; some sort of sacred summing-up formula, enabling him (at least here and now) to hold together in one all the immeasurable richness of the reality of Christ presented to him in the history of the Church, its devotion and its theology.

There do exist such primary words of invocation, comprehensive, unifying words, in which (so far as is possible to a creature, which is bound at the same time to be going out of itself into a real plurality) everything can be gathered together in one and "assimilated." Such primary words of devotion and theology can change; they can cease to be unifying, primary words, by which everything is invoked in one act, and turn into part-words. And, on pain of falling a prey to unhistorical arrogance, it is never possible to say of any word that it will remain such a primary, comprehensive word for ever. (Logos was once no doubt such a word for John himself, in which his whole theology is as it were summed up, but today it has become just one theological key-word amongst many; Christ as Sophia, as Gnosis, as the Son of Man, as "Spirit," may once have been other such words.) But woe to that age which no longer has any such magically unifying word, no word in which it can hear all things reconciled in a single unity. Its thinking and striving become formless, chaotic and disintegrated, its discourse (however true it may still be) turns to an unharmonious talking at cross-purposes, because it diverges in all directions, lacking a unifying unity. If it be said that "God" or "Jesus Christ" is itself precisely such a word, this would be right in the sense that such a word could, in the abstract, essentially and non-historically, be so. But this would be to overlook the fact that these two words (to take them as examples) cannot, in the concrete historical situation in which we and they are situated, be comprehensive and uniting words for the multiplicity of belief, devotion and theology, because they themselves are part of what needs to be gathered together and united, since one of them has to be given its full content while the other, its fullness being already deployed and itemized, has to be given unity.

And now, supposing we ask ourselves quite humbly where in the Church today such a primary, comprehensive and uniting word is to be heard. From what has here been said, it cannot simply be invented, for the fact that it is intrinsically possible for there to be many such words precisely does not mean that we can choose any we please, since what is historical is both what is contingent and that with which we are inescapably confronted. If we put this question, it will hardly be possible for us to point to more than one that really does have resonance and of which we may have at least some sense (if our experience goes no further) that it could perhaps reach to the center of our being and gather all things together in itself: and that one is HEART. Or what other is there to which you can point? Can anyone say "No, listen, there's another all-embracing, uniting word already being uttered—you just haven't been hearing it"? This word has got to be a naming of Christ, source of unity, in whom alone God is near to us (and in whom alone the word of God strikes a Christian note of help coming to us in the misery of our existence). But it will not do simply to call this Christ by his own name, since that word on its own is itself in need of a unifying center to gather together the multiplicity into which it has been expounded in the course of Christian history. At least, this is so for the mass of people in the Church in our time, and we do not need now to concern ourselves with other times, nor to assert apodictically that what applies to the many applies to all.

Apart from this word of the "Heart of Jesus," what word is there that both names the one and all-uniting Lord and at the same time unifies and interiorizes all the riches of him whom it names? There is none, no other has rung out but this one. But this one has been taken up by the devout and prayed and whispered and shouted from the rooftops (oh, yes, with a lack of discretion, often enough, that has been in horribly bad taste; but the self-offering of love cannot easily be made commensurable with taste and discretion). And the Church has accepted it. And she has said that she knows no other such word. Even if we were to say that this word is only one of many possible ones, and that tomorrow there will be another (issuing from the fullness of Christ) which will speak to men's hearts, saying all things in one and, having gathered them together, then send them out into multiplicity again; even if it be said that the modern Church's pronouncements about devotion to the Heart of Jesus are not made with any regard to the historical index of such words suggested here—all this would make no difference to our situation: only this word of the Lord's Heart can (if any can) be the word for which we are seeking, and which, even though it is there, we are also capable of missing, ignoring and rejecting.

What is invoked is that Heart which is the innermost thing and the unifying thing; the mystery which defies all analysis; the silent law which is mightier than any organization or utilitarian technique of man. What is named is that place in which the mystery of man opens into the mystery of God; empty infinity, becoming aware of itself, calls out to God's infinite fullness. It is the pierced Heart that is invoked, the anguished, exhausted Heart, the Heart that has died. That which is named here signifies love, the love that is unthinkable and selfless, the love that conquers in utter failure, that triumphs when it is powerless, that gives life when it is killed; the love that is God. This word proclaims that God is near to the one who prays, "My God, why hast thou forsaken me?" It speaks of what is utterly bodily and yet is all in all, so that we can count the heartbeats and know, weeping for joy, that we need go no further, for we have found God. Is it possible to deny that what we encounter in this word is ourselves, our present destiny, and the real meaning of being a Christian, something that is laid upon us as a burden and also as a grace, and entrusted to us as a mission? The real character of a particular age is not on the whole what is most familiar (which is rather what commonplace public knowledge has made of yesterday) but what is denied and yet ordained. And what could this possibly be today, if not the need and the task of rediscovering the Heart, and of bearing the burden of our own hearts, with their loneliness, their night of unhappiness, their anxiety at the thought of God?

How, then, should we give a *summa* of what it means to be a Christian other than by saying that God's eternal Word, sprung from the heart of the Father, has sought out our own heart, suffered it to the end, and will keep it forever?

If what has been said here is true concerning this primary word which gathers together and makes one, and which can be called the *summa* of all our devotion (as it is by Pius XI and Pius XII), then there follows a double conclusion: we must treat it with reverence, and hence with sober moderation; and we must learn to understand it as that primary word of power which gathers all things together.

We must treat it with sober moderation. The material to be gathered together and unified has first got to be there. This word is not, then, amongst the "elementary doctrines of Christ" (Heb. 6, 1). For we must first begin by going out into all the breadth and fullness of that which is later to be made one. And it is necessary that this initial going out shall be continually repeated, because otherwise we are constantly apt to lose, unawares, what we have already attained. Even the word Heart would become an empty, used-up formula without a continual searching of the Scriptures for the content of the Christian message, and silent hours of meditation on it, and the utterance of it in preaching. We cannot always, in all this, be speaking of "the Heart." This word, of the Heart of Christ, can retain its weight and its special function only on condition that it is not, by an excess of "pious" zeal, automatically used whenever we have anything to say about Jesus Christ. It should only be spoken and invoked by us when we are precisely concerned with speaking of the inward man, the "hidden person of the heart" (1 Peter 3, 4; cf. Rom. 7, 22; Eph. 3, 16 f.), in Christ (because we are faced with his incomprehensible fullness) and in us (because we are faced with our own empty disintegration). This is not something that arises on any and every occasion, important as it may sometimes be (and as it was for our Lord himself, who spoke, sparingly indeed but at crucial points, of our hearts and of his: Mt. 5, 8; 11, 29; 22, 37 etc.).

Secondly, a word like this has to be really understood. It is not the kind of word that simply states a "concept." True, every concept has some point at which it is open to the infinite, transcends itself and communicates with all things. True, every word (if it is more than a mere animal signal) has a resonance that goes beyond what it states conceptually, being always suspended in the incomprehensible. But in the case of most words, this matter of their openness to the incomprehensible does not arise; they are mostly concerned with conveying firmly and clearly what can be conceptually grasped. But the life of primary words[1] consists in their being open, and their laying us open, to the unutterable mystery of God (the God, in this case, who is an inconceivably loving intimacy). When they no longer do this, they may still express a concept, but as primary words they have died (a more terrible death than that of the body). But it is thus that they die in our minds when they are heard and spoken as concepts. For they are then simply not understood as they need to be understood. We say, indeed, of most of the key-words in our religious language, that what they name is a mystery. But if we are not, in the very saying of the word, aware of this mystery, if we do not let it be present to us, but stop short at what we do understand of the content of the word, discarding and ignoring, as merely not understood and not grasped, all that goes beyond this and in fact contains the mystery, instead of allowing this mystery to take possession of *us*, who can never for our part grasp *it*; if we flinch from stepping out of the word's small circle of light into its huge and holy darkness, then we kill it as a primary word and weaken it into a word with which the unholy, the undedicated and the loveless (plenty of whom are to be found amongst theologians) can equally well be on familiar terms.

But how is one to avoid weakening and killing these primary words? How is one to understand them as they ought to be understood; how are they to remain what they originally are? It is obvious from what has just been said that it cannot simply be a matter of enriching their conceptual content, "filling" them with anything, not even with a notional (as opposed to "realized") "inconceivability" or "infinity." To grasp what has to be done (which is not the same thing as doing it; and grasping it consists precisely in realizing that this is something that cannot really be grasped except by doing it, that action is here the only proper mode of knowledge) we have to think of it this way: while we focus on what is explicitly uttered, there comes gently down upon us, from behind as it were, the mystery by which this particular idea lives, upon which we are directly focusing. This is the way in which the mystery is present to us, not by talking about it as about the direct object of our statement: not in grasping it, but in being grasped by it. This is not a matter of "feeling" or unverifiable pious emotion, but of something without which all concepts would themselves be left in unintelligible isolation, something which belongs as such to cognition itself and sustains it: that quality, itself non-conceptual and non-objective, by which the mind is inherently *referred* to what is incomprehensible and unutterable but is made present, unuttered, in this very quality. It is possible (we are doing it now) to talk *about* this relatedness by which we are laid open to mystery, but it itself, in its own operation, is, initially and *per defini-tionem*, not present as when "grasped," for discussion pur-poses, in a strange sort of concept; it is present to a true act of cognition as a *being grasped*, wordlessly, by the incon-ceivable.

In itself, this is something which could be powerfully and sufficiently conveyed by all words, being that by which they all live; and such, perhaps, was the language of Para-dise, the all-embracing Whole ringing clear, and lovingly taking hold, in every word. In most of our words this quality of relatedness is repressed by our cramped and anxious cling-ing to "*idea clara et distincta*," though all of them are bound, as part of our own "conversion," to undergo a certain restora-tion in the direction of that paradisal symphony in which all things do indeed sound together in one whole—in the one *Word* of God. But there are some of our words which seem to be already further advanced in this conversion and return to their origin. And amongst them seems to be the word heart. Only when we have understood it in this way shall we have understood it as it really needs to be understood if it is not to become just one more trite word in our religious lan-guage, in which realities are merely expressed by concepts, without becoming present in the true realization of tran-scendence communicated by grace.

We have already said that the Heart of Jesus is a name for that reality in which the nameless mystery, whom we call God, is present, not as mysteriously withholding himself, but as pitying, self-giving intimacy: present where we are, in the central source of our earthly being, the heart. We then tried to say, further, that when we speak the name of this Heart we have to understand it in such a way that it can really be for us what it is in itself; so that the saying of this word can effect what it says in us; so that we can say it with understanding, and be of one mind with it. If this word is indeed to remain a primary word (and only then can it fulfill that gathering-together and unifying function of which we spoke at the beginning, without which there would be no point in it or in any special cult of the Heart of Jesus), then it has got to be understood in the way indicated here: not only as a conceptual statement, but with all of the strength of an actualization, coming forth from the center, of that grace-endowed relation of our minds to the very mystery of which this word is a name.

If, after the series of statements in the last paragraph, anyone still has difficulty in understanding what is meant, he can try to arrive at it from a different angle. In any religious concept, we have God given to us in a double way: in the meaning of what is said, conceptually and objectively presented; and in the very transcendence itself by which this act is sustained, which strains towards and points towards God. In any conceptual act performed under the influence of grace, by the "light of faith," this double quality in what is given is intensified: the objective content is now present both as something given revelation, in the *fides ex auditu*, and in a supernaturally elevated transcendence, no longer merely an openness to Being in general but a directing of the spiritual dynamics of the human person towards the final end of the *visio beata*, and (as *gratia increata*) the very reality of that which is believed already communicated to this person. This spiritually and pneumatically elevated and divinized transcendence of the human person does not objectivize itself, but this does not mean that it is simply unconscious, the mere mechanics of a mindless apparatus in the mind. It is non-objectively communicated to consciousness; it provides that unutterable, mysteriously wordless Plus, without which a religious concept cannot become truly itself.

Anyone who, in studying the metaphysics of knowledge, has come to a good Thomist understanding of the *lumen intellectuale* and the *objectum formale* of the mind; anyone who, in theology, has got the point of what is, because of the ontological elevation of such acts, the formal object of every supernatural act and of no other; anyone who takes seriously the teaching of Scripture concerning the anointing with the Holy Spirit, which teaches all things, and the "sighs too deep for words" of that Spirit who, as the Spirit of God who searches all things, is given to us—anyone to whom any of this applies cannot very well dispute that in a valid religious act this Plus is indeed present (consciously, though not immediately subject to reflection). But this Plus, this silent relation of openness to the meaning of the faith in the very performance (and not merely in the object) of the act itself, can make itself more clearly felt, be more existentially appropriated. That which we call spiritual consolation in the high point of the soul in faith, hope and love is what is meant by this higher, deeper, existentially more "radical" awareness of the meaning of the faith. It is in this awareness that we need to speak the word of the "Heart of Jesus," and it is thus that it should become clearer to us that all religious discourse (if it is to be utterly true and valid) needs to spring from such a realization. It is only thus that this word of the Heart of Christ can be saved from sinking to the level of so many other trite and commonplace religious words. It is to be used only sparingly. But when we utter it, when we wish to bring together all the rest of what we say of God's grace and compassion in Christ, and interiorize it and unite it within ourselves by speaking quietly and discreetly of the Heart of Jesus, then we must utter it in such a way that the bare word will be "understood" in this higher sense, the sense in which we shall understand all the words of the faith only when the eternal light of unclouded glory shines upon us.

Note

[1] On this concept, and what follows, cf. K. Rahner, *Schriften zur Theologie*, III (2nd ed., Einsiedeln, 1957), pp. 379-90 (on the prologomena to a theology of devotion to the Sacred Heart) and pp. 105-9 (on the experience of grace).

7

Ignatian Spirituality and Devotion to the Heart of Jesus

Canisius College is a Jesuit-run institution. It keeps the feast of the Sacred Heart as its patronal feast-day, and is concerned in other ways as well to promote devotion to the Heart of Jesus amongst its members. Given these two circumstances, the Canisian spirit cannot but be essentially determined both by Jesuit—or let us say, less off-puttingly, Ignatian, spirituality—and by devotion to the Sacred Heart. So it can hardly be out of place to ask ourselves, in these three preparations for meditation to be given today, tomorrow, and the day after, what the relationship is between these two essential constituents of the spirit of this house. So as to be able to think about this question, we must start today with a few thoughts about the special character of Ignatian spirituality in itself.

Characteristics of Ignatian Spirituality

I. There are a few unavoidable preliminaries before we shall be in a position to sketch the theme itself.

1. The older an Order is, the more difficult it is for it to keep its original spirit. This is simply part of the law of finitude in every creature. If we rebel in the wrong way against this fact, or ignore it, all we prove is that we are lacking in the

humility of the creature before God, whose life alone is unchangeable. All things grow old. Even the Church, though she (and she alone) has God's promise that she will still be living when all aging, *senescente mundo,* comes to an end, and God bestows his own eternal youth upon his creation. Growing old is not a merely negative concept. It is possible to grow wiser and more mature in old age, more serene and humble, looking with clearer sight and greater longing towards the one Kingdom of God. But if we consider this principle, if *we,* the Jesuits of today, consider it, then we have to ask ourselves, modestly and humbly, whether our lives, as lived in your sight, are both an adequate demonstration that we have the Ignatian spirit and a sufficiently intelligible representation of it to you. This is a question in its own right. It needs to be posed by us, not really by you. Hence I would like to ask you not to use these meditations as an examination of conscience for us, which would not be very useful to you yourselves. There will be something at least of the spirit of St. Ignatius still amongst us. It is better for you to ponder on that spirit itself than to ask yourselves whether we have it and are representing it properly.

2. There is only one Christianity. And in any legitimate living of it, it has to be present in its totality. Hence it does not make sense to demonstrate (since the fact is self-evident) that some particular feature claimed as characteristic of itself by some particular school or line of thought or Order in the Church is also to be found elsewhere. For while the whole of Christianity must obviously be present at each point in it, the entelechy of the whole structure being vitally discernible in every part of the achitectural plan, yet there are various schools and various spiritualities, differentiated by shifts in

accentuation, by what is stressed or unstressed, by variations in the dosage, by differences of perspective: in a word, by their historical individuality.

3. It cannot be disputed that today these differences within the Church, at least as regards the historical situation immediately confronting us, are being to a considerable extent obliterated and levelled out. This has its good side and its damaging side. I do not want to go any further here either into the fact of this general levelling down and smoothing out of the differences between ascetical schools, nor into what is valuable in it, nor into what is regrettable about it. Seen as a whole, the fact is part of our inescapable destiny as people living at this particular time; a destiny which we have to accept as the will of God, while striving so far as we can to assimilate what is good in this situation—the wealth of possibilities which it offers of participating in so many experiences of the Church's life and history—and to avert from ourselves what is damaging in it—a dull and drab uniformity, without sharp relief or vital energy.

4. Something follows from this where you yourselves are concerned. If God has arranged—positively or permissively—for you to become priests, or at least to travel some part of your way towards that blessed and frightening calling, here in this particular place, then this exposure to a milieu essentially constituted by Ignatian spirituality and devotion to the Sacred Heart is part of your destiny. Your best way of dealing with it is not to do all you can to ignore and dodge it, but to look at it, master it in the right way, and build it positively into your lives in whatever way corresponds to your own character and vocation. For it is clearly for this that God has let these things be present in your lives. One

must set about doing something positive with one's life. To react by shamming dead is not, generally speaking, the right way to deal with an inescapable situation. It seems to me that this makes the subject of these meditation-points meaningful for all of you. Even for those whose background, mental stamp, or membership of some particular Order requires them to have some other spirit. In the kingdom of the Spirit of God, the one Spirit who gives to each his particular gift and yet remains one, fidelity to one's own gift is not by any means the same thing as lack of interest in or refusal to learn from the other gifts of other schools, which are the workings of the same Spirit. It can happen that a more ancient school can find its way back to its own sources only by a route passing through more recent manifestations of our one Christianity.

II. The essential features of Ignatian spirituality. It is not possible to do more than point out some of them. And even someone who is genuinely representative of this spirituality may well feel that he finds this description incorrect. There is no way of avoiding this. Let me repeat that a characterization of this sort must deal with prevailing tendencies which, in actual performance and the common-sense processes of daily living, are constantly running in counterpoint with the opposite tendencies. Hence it does not make sense to contradict a characterization of this sort by saying that on the other hand it must not be overlooked that, etc., etc. Especially since, whenever such points come up, we have to ask whether the thing for which "equal" stress is demanded is being stressed because it is a real basic characteristic, or the opposite of one, needing to be stressed because otherwise the real characteristic in question would turn into a destructive force.

1. The first characteristic of Ignatian spirituality is certainly indifference. Indifference does not of course here mean simply the maxim that one must be ready to do the will of God, and hence be always prompt to detach one's heart from anything debarred by God's command or by one's destiny as dependent upon him. Indifference means more than this, for it could not, of course, be in any way a special characteristic of one particular spirituality. By indifference is here meant an extremely alert, almost over-acute sense of the relativity of all that is not God himself; of all things distinct from God as preliminary, needing to be passed through, expendable, ambiguous. Religious things included, for they too are not God. They too—that is, any particular exercises and methods, all the various devotions, practices, well-tried procedures and attitudes, all the established patterns in which the basic religious act of absolute self-surrender to God gives itself concrete shape, and must do so if it is not to fade away into vagueness and dissipate itself in a vacuum—they are all included in this non-distinguishing indifference. They are all subject to this almost lethal law that everything other than God is provisional, subject to cancellation, liable to be other than it is; permanently subordinate to God's ordinance, which is something that cannot be unambiguously discerned by looking at the thing itself and its permanent structures, and which can well be otherwise tomorrow than what it is today.

This indifference can never identify God with any particular way, any particular experience coming from him or leading towards him. God is always greater than what we know of him, and greater than the things which he himself has willed. His holy will, that to which absolute allegiance is given, is never precisely identical with any thing willed by him. The particular thing that is embraced as the realization of the will of God is always subject to the proviso, penetrating to the very core of its being, that this is "If, because, and so long as God pleases." This kind of indifference is coolly and, if you like, voluntaristically calculating. Hence comes what has often been adversely criticized as secular-minded rationalism, a superficial sort of training of the will, a failure to do justice to man's many-levelled complexity and creative and spontaneous forces. In small-minded men who also happen to be Jesuits, deep-rooted failures and deficiencies in regard to human potentialities can indeed camouflage themselves in a mere imitation of the Ignatian spirit. But when the spirit is genuine, all these things that are regarded as bad or dangerous in Jesuits are growths from a much deeper root: indifference. The experience—a monstrous and deadly dangerous experience —of how fearfully relative everything is except the One who is nameless and unutterable, who does not enter into any human reckoning, and beside whom everything great and everything holy, even though willed by him himself under the loftiest sanctions of his revealed will, is small and relative. This to the extent that there is only a very abstract (though important) sense in which things have an absolutely unambiguous hierarchy of values amongst themselves; in the concrete, there is nothing that might not be otherwise.

A small example illustrates this. Francis of Assisi refused to spare his eyes by guarding against the divine gift of tears, saying that after all eyes were something which he and flies had in common. Ignatius, while setting a high value on this mystical gift, kept up a defensive barrier against it, an attitude which, while seeming rationalistic and voluntaristic, sprang in fact from an ultimate, almost grim preoccupation with God alone: because it was conceivable that one might be better able to serve God by still preserving the poor gift of one's eyesight. His desire was to find God in all things. But this means that he was aware that even the most sublime and religious things are not God. Thus even his love of the cross, while present in the Exercises, is nevertheless immersed in this same ice-cold fire of indifference. We might (if such a concept happens to be meaningful to us) say that Ignatius is a man of transcendental rather than categorical spirituality.

2. Hence springs a second characteristic of the Ignatian mentality. I am prepared to describe this one with the fashionable word "existential." The indifferent man is not so much an individualist as is the Renaissance man, who sets a value on the lofty, unique, individual richness of his own personality and defends it as of high if not supreme worth. Ignatius has not, at bottom, much connection with the Renaissance, frequent as have been attempts to explain him in terms of it. An understanding of the world which is reached as the fruit of a mystical death, and in which everything can be held valuable because there is not very much value in anything, makes him precisely the opposite of the men who arrived at a new love of the world in the Renaissance, in which the mysticism of the absolute was within an ace of perverting itself into the world itself. He is an individualist in that both kinds of things, both the common and the exceptional, both what lies near at hand to man and to the good things of the world and what is remote from them, have equally become as it were of secondary rank before God, who, while willing the existence of both, does not absolutely identify himself with any, and cannot wholly be found in either. This makes Ignatius the individualist not of personality but of the person, and possibly,

according to circumstances, of the poor rather than the rich person; the person soberly doing his job and putting himself in order; the person who knows his vocation to come from the immediate will of God, who disposes of a person in this way or that, always keeping him on call, never showing more than a brief stretch of the way before him, always requiring him to remain open to the God who is greater than anything that has yet been experienced of him; a God who can disclose himself as well in emptiness as in fullness, in life as in death; who can be found in the exterior and interior riches whether of the cultural or religious man as well as in the emptiness of poverty.

Hence the sceptical, disillusioned, here-and-now, calculating, planning character, the acceptance that things can be otherwise, the occasional seeming disloyalty, the adaptability and all that kind of thing which, for good or ill, makes up the Jesuit character. This attitude of disillusionment, or regarding things as interim and provisional, this faint scepticism, this pressing into service of everything that is not God himself, and along with this the readiness to meet each unique, fresh situation and the fresh summons ever being made in it—uniqueness experienced not as riches but as service, as a responsibility which cannot be evaded by fleeing into the commonplace nor perverted into an enjoyment of one's own special richness—all this is what I want to call the existential quality. To my mind, it is so characteristic of Ignatius that I dare to think, on this ground, that he belongs to the future, not to an age now coming to an end; that this is a character not of the modern age now ending but of the age to come, though it remains to be seen whether those who, historically, call themselves his disciples and pupils will be the ones who really represent this spirit in the future.

3. The third characteristic of Ignatian spirituality is its relation to the Church. Every age loves the Church and draws its life from her. But in Ignatius there is a *reflexive consciousness* of the Church's presence: the Church which is to be served in spite of all one's experience of its weaknesses. This Church is the *ecclesia militans*, the Papal Church, and thus the Church in its most unambiguous visibility. No one will dispute that this is an essential characteristic of Ignatian spirituality. One could of course consider the question of whether this is a fundamental trait equal with the two already named or whether what we have here is a necessary counterpoint to the other two. But perhaps it comes ultimately to the same thing. For he who has truly experienced God's absolute transcendence, really meaning God and not the sublime enjoyment of his immeasurable and transcendent self, will be the first to let himself be humbly and naturally directed by God into the limits laid down for him; he will simply and humbly accept whatever finite thing may be willed by God, though it is not God, including whatever relative distinctions God has willed to make between these things, making them in a certain sense absolutes for any creature who does not aim to make himself God. Hence that unconditional love for the humanity of Christ, for his earthly life in all its concrete limitation, for the Church, the Church's hierarchy, the Pope, the rules governing our attitude to the Church. Not that there is any fanatical, optimistic tendency to identify any of these things with God. Ignatius, who admitted that all his bones shook within him at the election of Paul IV, was very far from anything of that sort. His relation to the Church

is the humility of the creature who does not make an idol of himself, nor of his own mysticism and immediate relationship with God, and is therefore ready to accept the finite thing which God has established to represent him within the finitude of creation. The root from which grows this relationship to the Church is the silent love of humility, of service, of lack of self-importance, which is thus both the product and the antitoxin of existential indifference.

We must stop. Do not forget that I have been describing characteristics which are never found on their own in a state of chemical purity, and would be lethal if they were. I must leave it to you to consider whether, in the actual life which you live in this house, you can find an everyday embodiment of this spirit, or whether you can discern nothing of it whatsoever. What we must think about in the next series of points is how devotion to the Sacred Heart is at once the fruit of this spirit and its defense against its own dangers.

Devotion to the Sacred Heart as the Interior Counterbalance to Ignatian Spirituality

In our first meditation, we tried to consider the special character of Ignatian spirituality. As with everything else, a particular spirituality of this sort is something which, in most of its features, and the most important ones, coincides with others, differing from them only in a few less important things (though this is only a crude statement of a true and important point). Our business has been to speak of the features which distinguish this spirituality from others. Not of those in which it is at one with others: love of God, grace, the reality of our Lord, and many other things which are common to all types of spirituality, though even what they have in common may be stamped with their own particular character and thus modified.

We must not, then, forget that what is special is not the whole nor even the most important. And hence it should not be surprising if we also need to say that what is special is sometimes highly dangerous if taken on its own in a chemically pure state, as it were. We can see how even at the biological level the characteristic structure of a species may develop to such a point of bizarre exaggeration that the species destroys itself by overspecialization. There is something of the same sort in the spiritual order. In this respect, humility is a kind of prophylactic against the self-destructive excess of any particular school. It is by remaining humbly open to other ways that one keeps safely within the bounds which alone make it possible for the finite to reach limitless perfection. Clearly, then, any healthy spirituality, any that is duly moderate, non-heretical, humbly ready to set bounds to its own special characteristics, is inevitably going to construct within itself a further element as part of its own special character, to act—odd as it may sound—as a protection against itself: thus producing an equilibrium of opposing forces within which its own special, primary characteristics can be a blessing and not a destructive force.

If we think back to what I was saying yesterday about the special character of Ignatian spirituality, there will be no need to linger over what is dangerous and threatening about it. If not protected against itself it can be rationalistic, cold, calculating, sceptical, icy, exaggerating the relativism of all things other than God to such a point of non-committedness that there is no longer any possibility of seeing and engaging

with either earthly or religious things in accordance with
what they themselves truly are. Indifference can become perverted into a deadly sort of functionalism, an infinite adaptability capable of everything and hence of nothing. God can
become so transcendent, so nameless and formless, that he
becomes as it were an empty word, and the thing that is really
hiding under that word becomes after all (though anonymously) something that is very much not God: our own organization, the power of the Church, the functioning of the
machine for its own sake, statistics of practicing Catholics
(never mind just how they are doing it) etc. The dangers
in the emphasis on the Church are well known: the Church
is transformed from an instrument in the hand of God to
an end in itself; the Church is identified with one particular
tendency, school of thought, or attitude; only those are
counted loyal to the Church who are of the same opinion as
ourselves. The existential ascetic turns into a man who has
himself so perfectly under control that he has everything
—except a heart to be aware of its own abandonment to the
will of God, a heart to laugh and weep as life, and not he
himself, dictates.

I am now going to propose the view that devotion to the
Sacred Heart of Jesus is the requisite antitoxin, produced out
of Ignatian spirituality itself, to these dangers inherent in it
(dangers which grow in proportion to the depth of that spirit,
and to which the crude bourgeois is only too immune, which
is his loss). Let us think about this a little, for it is a line of
thought well calculated to take us further into the meaning
of devotion to the Sacred Heart. Let us note, first of all, that
the bare fact of a connection between Ignatian spirituality and
devotion to the Sacred Heart is shown by its having been the

Jesuits, or more accurately certain Jesuits, who were the first promoters of this devotion. This was so to such a degree that, unless one is prepared rationalistically to reduce Church history to a matter of mere chance, one cannot explain the connection simply by the fact that St. Margaret Mary Alacoque happened to have a Jesuit confessor and visionaries are apt to enlist their confessors, and the Orders to which they belong, as tools of their mission.

1. Indifference and the Heart of Jesus. Indifference has a great deal in common with death. We die to the world. Not only to the evil world in all its evil. This is meant to be a death which will prevent us from loving it in any sinful way, falling in love with it, mistaking it for God. But such a death, such a wintry fading of all things into a background of grey insignificance, can be deadly to a human being in a way which is not the death set by God between us and true life. It can mean the withering of the heart into a stale uncaringness which is no longer aware of any of the differences in things which God has in fact made and wills to have preserved. The death which is indifference can only be life-bearing when it is effected by love and is a dying into love. Indifference must not kill the heart, it must only be the death of that secret self-seeking which cramps us and rejects the infinite freedom of God. Indifference must be love. If it is stoic apathy, if it is at bottom the cowardice which surrenders because it despairs of victory, if it is a meanness of heart, blind to the magnificence of reality and the splendor of the world, then it is not true indifference.

But anyone striving for true indifference is always in danger of accepting the false kind, because it is easier and less painful to have than the true. This is why it is necessary for the

indifferent man to practice a cult of love, of burning, en-
thusiastic, reckless love. This is why he needs to be told and
told again that the center of the whole world and of all truth
is a heart: a burning heart, a heart which has laid itself open
to any fate that can befall, which has in fact undergone everything that fate can do, not taking refuge in the dead heart-
lessness of the man whom, because he is dead instead of having died into love, no burning fate can touch any longer.
Indifference must be a readiness of the heart to love, so far
as it can, *all* things rather than just this or that; not to be
uncaring towards all things. Indifference must learn to recognize itself in a heart that has been pierced through, and is
precisely thus living and life-giving. All that indifference is
really saying is that the perfect heart is the pierced heart, the
heart utterly poured out, the heart that does not shrink and
hold back from committing the whole of its love merely
because its love receives no answer. It is because this is true
love that there has to be the death of indifference. Otherwise
it would always be better to love *something* at least, rather
than have a heart burned to the ashes of uncaring cynicism
and call it by the lofty name of indifference. The sublime
gift of indifference is saved from being a deadly poison only
when it is received by someone with an adoring devotion to
love; someone who dares to have a heart being an adorer
of *the* Heart. And it can of course happen that such adoring
veneration is given to that Heart without the adoring lover's
ever having heard of devotion to the Sacred Heart of Jesus.

2. Devotion to the Sacred Heart is protection against the
danger inherent in the existential element in Ignatian spirituality. I used the word existential to describe the person
in that self-knowing, solitary, unique individuality which does

not seek to savor itself, to blossom out and grow rich, but allows itself to be used up in service, because it does not have much sense of its own importance but submits itself to the law of indifference. Now, an existential element of this sort must inevitably stand in danger of deadly lovelessness: hardness and (perhaps disguised) cynicism, that subtle form of contempt for human beings which, because it "knows what is in man," loves neither itself nor anyone else, the most it can rise to being a sort of weary patience with man and his human weakness. This existential quality is in danger of becoming solitary in a deadly sense: as though sightless, grey, burned-out at the heart, knowing far too much to be able to love. For this lonely individuality in its ultimate incommensurability is experienced as something finite and relative, not something rich and proud; it is as it were akin to that ultimate inability to feel any loving enthusiasm about anybody which leads to dreary bachelorhood, mistaking itself for virtuous celibacy and incensed by any weakness in this matter on anyone else's part. It is an attitude which is in danger of thinking that this sort of inability to let go of oneself is true and tested virtue, whereas the latter is in truth always the saving by grace of something in constant peril.

This existential element, solitary by its very nature and always in danger of frigidly congealing, can only be wholesome and good when it is adopted in humility by a heart that loves, loving another heart. Only someone who loves can bear with himself and others for long, without despising himself and them. Only someone who loves can see himself in his own uniqueness, and do the same for someone else, without finding his own and the other person's limitations sticking in his throat, without feeling that he has "had enough of it." It is very difficult not to hate oneself, said Bernanos. It is impossible except by loving; by loving that Heart, in the concrete, which is the Heart of Christ. For even the man who knows himself, upon whom the burden of his own self is laid without any protective screen around it, must, if he is going to be able to deal with himself, forget himself; but he cannot forget himself by plunging into his own emptiness. How is he to do it without losing himself? How is he to manage it, except by loving? How can anything draw him out and away from himself, so to say, out of his emptiness and lack of sure foothold, unless it be something that he loves? For otherwise it cannot draw him; if it is unloved it can only intensify the pain of his finitude and relativity.

But if there has to be such love, and such ultimate love, for what is finite; if, again, love is that which is unconditioned; if, then, it would seem to be almost paradoxical to love unconditionally that which is conditioned; then the ultimate guarantee of the possibility of such a love is offered when unconditioned, infinite love has taken something finite to itself in absolute, unsurpassable love, and absolutely identified itself with it. But this is what happened when God took the finite humanity of Christ to himself as his own reality; took the finite center of a human reality to himself, in that act of love which was the hypostatic union, so really, so absolutely, so unconditionally that this reality is for all eternity his own, really participating in an unsurpassable way in the absoluteness of God, without ceasing to be finite in itself; belonging to him in such wise that it would be a relativizing of God himself if one were to try, existentially and lovelessly, to relativize that reality which he assumed.

This is why any genuine love for any finite being in its

unconditioned reality in the concrete order is a loving directed towards the Heart of Christ; it has an incarnational character; it is a hidden kind of faith (or a preliminary form of it) in the incarnation, and hence a form of devotion to the Sacred Heart. A person who has come consciously to himself can no longer, perhaps, love so naively, so straightforwardly, as others can; he needs a love which opens onto infinity, because the finite on its own would be too much of a disappointment, unbearable in its insignificance. But if love is not to be perverted into a proud savoring of one's own measureless and never-satisfied demands for "all or nothing," then, despite its boundless character, it must be a love of the infinite made concrete, giving love the freedom of the infinite and yet allowing to all other concrete realities their place and rank beside it, as also worthy of love. And this can only be the concrete Heart of the infinite God, the divine-human Heart. A man who can no longer return to the naive state preceding the shock of reality, a man who has really been confronted with his own existence, will only escape being paralyzed by this gazing into death if he knows with the utmost power of faith and hope that he is loved, in the concrete, by one whose love cannot be relativized into a childish, superficial illusion, because it is the love of God, the love of his Heart.

3. Is there any need to dwell on the fact that radical loyalty to the Church can only be sound and wholesome when it is the loyalty of a heart serving in love, a heart whose relationship to the Church is loving? Whenever a servant of the Church is a man lacking in love, his Church turns itself into a collective egoism in which "God" and "the salvation of souls" are the words used, while the power and prestige of the

Church and of himself are the things meant. Ecclesiastical office can only be defended by those who are loving, and who defend it while giving loving service. Truth is only luminous when it glows with the warmth of love. Men will only come to the sacraments if they can see that they have had that effect in the one who administers them which is the only effect at which, fundamentally, they aim: *caritas Dei diffusa est in cordibus*. Only those who love can make of the Church they serve that which she is meant to be (and this is the only true way to serve her): the means, in humble service, of salvation for all.

If we cannot help sometimes getting the feeling that we are living in a state of siege; that we are merely one party amongst many, one historical tradition amongst many; that, along with what cannot be surrendered (cannot, for the reason of love: love precisely of the others), we would also be prepared to defend our own habits, our own particular inheritance, because it is more comfortable that way and we happen to be obstinate and proud; if we often have to ask ourselves whether we are really prepared to be all things to all men, whether we are prepared to take the initiative in approaching the minds of others, or only to wait graciously, in our self-assured self-satisfaction, for them to approach us —do we not then need to ask ourselves whether we have prayed enough for the grace to be humbly and self-forgetfully loving, to be tender-hearted, to be people who forget themselves in order to serve others? And what better way could there be of praying for this grace, where better could we learn the humility needed for loving (love is humbling: to the non-loving person, looking at it from outside, it always seems something stupid and unmanly), where better than in the Heart of our Lord, who loved and was not ashamed to love? It is only those modest people who have the ability to recognize their *own* narrowness, and not only that of others, who can manage not to degrade the rules of loyalty to the Church into narrow-minded, narrow-hearted party fanaticism without even noticing it; it is only those capable of really loving who can really love the Church. For she, the Bride of the Lord, wearily and in poverty pursuing her pilgrimage through time and ever longing for the marriage of the Lamb, desires to be loved; but it is not possible for a person to love her who identifies himself with her like a party fanatic with his party, a man who at bottom does not love at all, but hates.

It is not possible to say, in discussing the special quality of one particular spirituality, that its peculiar characteristic is love. For this is the thing that is common to all. The special character of a spirituality must reside in other gifts, such as can be variously and singly distributed. But of all these gifts it can be said that if I have them ". . . and have not love, I am nothing." This, then, applies equally to the special character of Ignatian spirituality. But the ultimate source of love is the Heart of our Lord. And hence Ignatian spirituality can only be healthy if it loves that Heart and loves in union with it. Otherwise all that is most sublime in it becomes most deadly.

Ignatian Spirituality as a True Flowering of
Devotion to the Sacred Heart

We have tried to examine the special character of Ignatian spirituality and to ask why and how devotion to the Sacred

Heart constitutes a defense against those dangers which are inevitably bound up with that type of spirituality, in the same way that any other human characteristic has its built-in perils, since everything finite is, precisely, finite and hence insecure. But ultimately, only something that is part of the thing itself, genuinely related to it, can be a protection against the deadly danger that is built in to any finite thing. No alien thing could ever provide this safeguard. If this is true, then we can and must see the relationship between Ignatian spirituality and devotion to the Sacred Heart not merely in terms of the one being insecure and in danger, and the other the thing that saves it, but also in terms of devotion to the Sacred Heart, rightly understood, as the real context and source from which springs this special character of Ignatian spirituality, and for this reason providing it with the safeguard it needs. Thus the ultimate thing is not the opposition between them but their unity. This unity manifests itself in the duality which we have been considering so far. This is something that needs to be seen. So we will ask ourselves why and how it is that the divine-human love which we adoringly venerate in the valid sign of the Heart of Jesus is of such a nature that it gives rise to the characteristics of Ignatian spirituality as its own characteristics and sustains and protects them in coexistence with itself.

1. Divine-human love. Love is always a going out of oneself, always the miracle of the surpassing of oneself. St. Thomas saw, profoundly, that knowledge is, in a sense, a transcendence which only draws in to oneself, a returning upon oneself, laden and enriched with all that reality has to offer, which is thus appropriated as one's own treasure. It is only in the second primary act of a spiritual, personal

being, which is love, that the greater miracle takes place: that making over of what is one's own to what is other than one-self—or, better, to him who is other, the beloved person. This necessarily involves, to begin with, a detachment from oneself, an indifference towards oneself, a trustful letting-go of oneself, an act of denial towards the anxious assertion of its own existence by the finite being, which always thinks it has got to watch out for itself, always supposes that it will lose itself unless it carefully looks after itself. But in this opening-out of spiritual and personal love (not a mere instinct going out of itself only to fall a prey to some other isolated being, and hence not free, more like collective egoism than love), the person who loves, whenever such love is real, and however much it may seem only to attach itself to some one individual, reaches to the Whole; he becomes free, he loves all things, not merely many individual things lumped to-gether, but the primal Whole: God.

But this means that this love itself, in its unquenchable radicality, becomes not only indifference towards the lover himself, but also indifference towards the separate individual as such. Not that it does not love the individual, the other. But it takes him into that endless movement in which all is loved, all is praised, all is recognized as glorious; and the name of this "all" that stands before and behind the sum-total of all the individual things and persons loved is simply God, so that it is truly the case that it is only possible really to love in so far as, in and beyond one's love (whether know-ingly or unwittingly), one is loving God.

Seen in this way, indifference is simply the openness of love (love of the individual object) to that "all" which is God, which it must preserve if it is truly to love that individual;

for lover and beloved would both die of their own finitude if both were not open to the one infinite fullness which is God, who has willed to be himself the fullness and infinity of finite being. Hence true indifference is the loving, positive relativizing of all finite individuals. It does not "expose" them in all their limited wretchedness; it does not "see through" them into the empty nothingness within. It sees their finitude only to recognize them in their relationship to the infinite (which is indeed relativity), to see them as held in the protective embrace of endless love. It breaks upon both its own heart and the self-enclosed rigidity of the thing it loves; it is hard enough and tough enough not to shrink from the death involved in that breaking-open. But it knows that it thus redeems them; that in the infinite love of the Infinite, every finite thing is itself made infinite.

For if it is true that anything loved is loved in so far as it is loved by God, and if this love of God for a finite person is the self-communication of God himself to the finite being in grace and glory, then the finite is loved as something that has been made infinite by grace, when it is loved with this love of God. Radical love is possible only in God, because only in him do all things communicate and give themselves to each other, so that everything can be loved as though it alone were everything. And this is exactly what love desires to do. Thus it itself becomes indifference. Indifference is simply that aspect of love in which, in its raising up of the world, it is moving with it through time and history towards the goal of "God all and in all," in which all that will remain is love and love alone. It needs also to be considered in this connection that in this "fallen" order of *sinfully* self-enclosed creatures and a self-assertive anxiety which is itself sin or at least arises out of sin, indifference as the opening of the creature to all-uniting love cannot but have a special, in some degree "bloody," character—the character of a heart that has been pierced. But let us leave that to your own meditations.

2. We now have to consider how love is, of its very nature, "existential" in the sense in which we have used this term to characterize Ignatian spirituality. There has never yet been any love which failed to regard itself as unprecedented and unique. Nor is this opinion which love has of itself mere silly imagining; where love is really love, it is really so. For love does indeed liberate us into what is special to ourselves. For when a man has entered into that love which embraces and sums up all things in itself, then there, and there alone, nothing can exist alongside him which could replace him, in the sense of having the same thing twice over. What he is is precisely that uniqueness which embraces the whole. And this uniqueness really is individual; loving precisely *like this* can happen only once. This particular point, from which there is a reaching-out to consent to and embrace the whole, can exist only once. Love is the birth of that true, ultimate individuality which is not a cramped solitariness but an image of those individualities in God which, unique in themselves (it is only by *us* that they are enumerated in conjunction with each other), each uniquely possesses the totality of the divine essence, while asserting and lovingly assenting to the individuality which is other than themselves.

Love, and love alone, is existential in yet another sense: it gives knowledge of one's own uniqueness in terms of vocation, task and mission. It is in action, in that being which is doing, not in the static being and mere words of conceptual objectivity, that a man arrives at that special individuality which he is meant to have. This applies to a man in a way which it does not to an angel (still less to God), because it is really by his own free decision that a man rises from being a mere particular instance of his species to unique, individual personality. But this unique act (which precisely does *not* consist merely in the repetition, case by case, of the kind of behavior demanded of all men by universal laws, precisely *not* in the mere embodiment of universal human nature, but is the simply unique) is liable to miscarry. It is possible for man to find his individuality in the uniqueness of his own guilt, his individual guilt, which again is something more than an offense against universal norms. If he does not wish to do this, where is he going to find that summons which declares to him, above and beyond all universal norms (however much they must indeed be observed), the task and the mission which save him from being a source of deathly weariness and desolation to himself? Is this something one creates out of the depths of one's own being? Though it does indeed come from one's inmost center, it is precisely not one's own in the sense of coming from one's own resources, but one's own in the sense of being given; that which is most one's own, because it is God's.

In other words, we discover the personal only as we go out to encounter that image of us which God has made for himself, the picture of us which he holds before us and by which we, imperfect as we are, are always simultaneously cast down and delighted, because we recognize in it both ourselves and our God. We can do no more than move towards it; it is only slowly revealed, and never wholly in this life. While we are still pilgrims, it is not only God but we ourselves too that we can know only in reflections and likenesses;

it is only *then* that we shall know ourselves, too, even as we are known. But we can already gather some hint of that special uniqueness which is the grace of God, who gives to everyone that which is uniquely his own and which makes him worthy to exist for ever.

But how are we to discover this task, this image, if it comes from God? It seems cheap and easy to say, in the unity of love with God. And yet it is so: it is only in love that we can understand God, and only thus that I can understand what he wants of me in particular. It is only in love for God that we can be ready to accept ourselves as he, in love, conceives of us. Otherwise the ultimate can only be, even in regard to ourselves, sheer despair, and protest even against ourselves; the discovery of our individuality only the discovery of our own special bottomless abyss.

It is no accident that the Exercises, rightly understood, are at one and the same time the discovery of love in Jesus Christ, for the God who is ever greater than we have known, and the discovery of our own individual image, our "vocation," in inspiration from above (and not in rational planning from below). But inspiration from above (which may be something very simple in its external happening) is only possible for a man who loves. For only then can he give his consent to God, in whom alone his own existence, in all its uniqueness, is to be found. When found in such love, of course, it is never in a self-savoring possession of it but in some service in which one forgets oneself, seeing oneself in the matter in hand, with which one identifies oneself. Here it must not be forgotten that our special, unique existence is a participation in the life of Christ, an imitation of our Lord and of his destiny renewed in such fashion that we are really continuing his life, not copying it for the *nth* time. And hence this Christian mission of ours, this special character, can only be discovered in love of the God-Man, a love in which we accept his love, in which he confers existence upon us.

3. Not much remains to be said on devotion to the Heart of Jesus as the source of true love for the Church. For the Church herself springs from that Heart. *Ex corde scisso Ecclesia Christo iugata nascitur*. This is a truth. For the Spirit without which the Church would be no more than an organization, no more than a synagogue, flows from the pierced Heart of Christ; it is the Spirit of recklessly prodigal love. But this is to say, too, that the true nature of the Church can be rightly understood only in terms of her origin. But it is only if we understand her nature aright that we can truly love the Church as she must be loved, and avoid the danger of meaning something quite different when we are seeking and desiring to love the Church. To see her as from our Lord's Heart, to love her from thence, to love her, by grace, in co-operation and imitation of that love which is her very foundation, is to love her with love like that which Paul described as the love of Christ for his Bride, the Church, and love as it was seen by the Fathers of the Church. It is *by* his love for sinful, lost humanity, thus purifying and redeeming it, that Christ constitutes it as the Church, his Bride; by his love, in which he loves mankind in spite of all, he takes this adulterous, God-forsaking mankind, and makes it his Bride; it is only his love that first makes her holy and worthy of love. Thus his love is always, so to say, playing back and forth between sinful humanity (which is still to be found within the Church as an empirical fact) and the Church who has been truly made holy.

If, then, our love for the Church is to be like Christ's, then this means that we must truly love men who are sinful and lost and searching for her; we must love a Church which is forever being made anew out of this humanity; we must be able to love a Church which is precisely *not* simply the holy, immaculate Bride of Christ without spot or wrinkle, but has got to become, in this patient, compassionate, enduring love, that which she is meant to be: the holy Bride of Christ. In this love we must even love ourselves, humbly and patiently loving those who are sinful, those who are full of failings, those who are making their own contribution to the sinful, bond-woman image of the Church. We must love a Church who cannot recognize herself as complete until everything which God has predestined for salvation has come home to her at last; and has come, not only to receive from the splendor of the Church, but also to bring with it all that these returning wanderers themselves have of the Spirit, of grace, of life, of special characteristics, of unique experience, so as to bring it back to that home which cannot be complete until they too are at home in it.

Thus love which proceeds from the Heart of Christ is ready to take risks, clearsighted, not preoccupied with defense of the Church, but concerned that the Church shall serve as did her Lord, who did not come to be served but to serve and to give his life for many. Love like this does not seek the honor of the Church but the salvation and honor of those who are meant to find the Church; seeing that so few do find it, it looks for the reason for this in ourselves, not in those outside. Love like this is missionary, not conservative and defensive. Love like this knows that the Church is always renewed at precisely that moment when "someone," his heart pierced, seems to go down in utter ruin and yet does not despair, but recognizes this hellish situation as the hour of his love, love of man and of the Father.

Throughout the discussion of these last three days we have been tacitly assuming, at the back of our minds, that the devotion to the Sacred Heart of which we were speaking would not necessarily and in all cases be a devotion explicitly set forth and delimited in the word "Heart." Otherwise, it would not have been legitimate to present this devotion as so closely and absolutely bound up with the most funda- mental things in Christianity and in our spirituality. But all that explicit devotion to the Sacred Heart is ultimately meant to do is to see to it that this Spirit of love flowing from the pierced Heart of Christ does indeed animate us. But if any- one is given the grace to name explicitly this thing which, however namelessly, belongs to the very essence of Chris- tianity, then this implies a new responsibility, which it is im- possible for you to avoid, and the promise of a blessing: may it be granted to us all to share in it. If we receive that bless- ing, then we shall understand how, in the death of indiffer- ence, we die in order to live; how we attain to our own lonely uniqueness only that we may, in love, discover the other per- son and serve him; and how we love the Church in order to love all men.

8

First Mass

In the course of these last two happy days God has already spoken within this house, and so has man. Yesterday God spoke the creative word which made these men priests. And today these priests spoke for the first time alone and on their own responsibility, the greatest word that a man can speak, the sacramental word in which God's highest act of love becomes the presence of salvation amongst us.

What is there that can be said after that? Most certainly, only something less than has been said already. Most certainly only a feeble echo of it, faint and a little blurred at best, in which a man can think over once again what he has already heard and spoken in its primary form. But it does make sense to do something of this sort. For we of this earth remain always people to whom what has already been heard and obeyed only fully comes home when it is thought over, reconsidered, and re-enacted in retrospect. Only when God speaks into us his final word, uttering himself to us directly in eternal life, shall we fully understand that word which has filled these past two days.

If one can dare to speak, then, after such words have been spoken, it can only be to say a word to these priests, a word to their parents and families, and a word to God.

A word to the priests who today have offered their first

sacrifice on the altar of Christ. Your first impression may be that this word sounds like an admonition, but this is really only in appearance. For on this day when the inner law of the priesthood has been given to you in all its fullness, the day when you have received the holy Spirit of the power and might of Christ's priesthood, on such a day anything that is said about the tasks and duties of the priesthood can only be a joyful extolling of its dignity, praise of God has given it to you, invocation of the Spirit in whose fellowship there is no law, who is the Spirit of freedom and blessed strength, and who never demands anything that he has not first already bestowed.

This inconceivably magnificent new honor that has been given you is the severely difficult honor of serving your brothers in the Church and in the world in the name of Christ. Nothing else at all. For this is the greatest of honors. You are not called to anything else. If anything else beyond this may come to be allotted to you in the Church of Christ, still all that will be asked of you before the judgment seat of God is whether in it too you have pursued and carried out the one calling that is yours: to be priests of Jesus Christ, witnesses of his truth, dispensers of his grace, lonely followers of the Crucified, servants of your brethren.

This call has come to you in a strange, twilight time, a time of which we cannot say whether its dubious tranquility is the beginning of an age of real peace or the calm before a storm in which God will winnow out his grain on the threshing-floor of world history more ruthlessly than he ever yet has done. Pray, then, and deny yourselves, so that you may be able to stand fast when the judgment of God begins at the house of the Lord.

Do not become satisfied citizens of a merely comfortable refrigerator-and-television civilization. This is something which, in the disguise of reasonableness and good sense, is threatening to infiltrate even amongst those who profess allegiance to the kingdom of God: a kingdom which is not to be found in earthly prosperity, but in hunger for righteousness, in tears of repentance, and in the expectation of a blessedness promised as an eternal reward only to the poor and persecuted. May faith in Christ crucified and the expectation of judgment and the eternal kingdom live in your hearts.

Defend the Church by pouring out your life in selfless love, fearlessly and with wide-open heart, in the service of all men; but never be conscious of being anything but unprofitable servants.

Preserve the Church's heritage of truth and experience while reaching out boldly to take hold on the future, which belongs to God precisely in the same way as the past. But do not look for the future in the world's programs, because that is not your affair; have a simple trust that if a Christian man will merely accept himself straightforwardly as he here and now is, in the Spirit given to him from God, then he will also be able to perceive what program he is to follow in whatever future he may be called upon to conquer or to endure.

When you defend the heritage of the past, it must not be out of lazy-mindedness or a false craving for security, but out of loyalty to the truth of God, ever ancient and ever new, to which you are bound. When you are striving for anything that is new, let it be done in humility and with serene courage, faithfully carrying out your true duty: something which does not always receive its reward on this earth by earthly recognition within the Church.

It is in Rome, in close proximity to the Pope, that you have become priests. This is something that it should be possible to discern in you. But the best way for it to be so is in the sheer integrity of your selfless service.

Try to be adaptable and many-sided. But do not think you can become universally competent and thus impress people. The only thing which can ultimately impress them in such a way as to further the gospel is the kind of faith which is ready to risk its life, and unfeigned love. If there is anyone who does not listen to you because you are less competent in the wisdom of this world than he, then he is not yet ripe for the grace of the kingdom of God. God will give him further help in his own good time.

Do not pretend that your faith is untroubled and without conflicts if in fact it is not so; but rather show to others, humbly and unaffectedly, what you really are. Show them how, in the midst of the darkness of this godless world, which weighs on you as it does on them, it is possible to be a man sustained in grace by faith and at the same time living that faith in the courageous freedom of a fearful heart. Do not fear the weariness, anxiety and leaden heaviness of futile helplessness in your pastoral life. These too are graces, for they give you a share in the agony of your Lord in the Garden of Olives, which must be suffered to the end throughout world history.

Hold fast to each other in brotherly love; vie with each other in mutual respect and helpfulness, honor each other's gifts and talents, even when they are not your own kind. For the one Spirit imparts to each a different gift, and the whole Body of Christ is never present in one single member. And even fighting for the right against a brother who is in the wrong does not justify the use of poisoned weapons, or an attitude which contradicts the spirit of the gospel.

Strike out boldly along new paths in pastoral work. But if these paths do not in the end lead to the altar of Christ, to the confessional and to the prie-dieu, they are not paths of Christ leading to life.

Together with your bishops, accept responsibility also for those Christians who do not belong to the Church of your priesthood. It is not possible to do what you are required to do for the one holy Church unless you try as well to learn from these Christians, since they too have a message to us from God and could well bring much with them into the one new household of God and his Christ, in which you have been set as servants over the People of God. Do not scandalize these Christians by your attitude, or by laying burdens upon them that are prescribed not by God but by you.

Your pastoral work among the poor must not be done as a safeguard against their becoming a threat to the Church's position of power. They are your brothers. This is the reason for your being sent to them. The starting-point of your work with them is not their class war. But neither must you take any part in the class war of the rich. This is not so easy to see. But which of us can say that he has not already been a beneficiary of a system which represents man's sinful disorder in organized form, rather than the order which comes from God?

You, unlike some, have not regarded your studies merely as an unavoidable obstacle to be surmounted on your road to ordination. But do not forget that these studies, begun in Rome, must end, not here, but only on your death-beds. This is easily said. The older we get, the less ready we are to learn,

either from books or from life. For you must realize that all
that boasted experience to which everyone is fond of appeal-
ing is as subjective as we sinners ourselves. Our experience
would often have been different if we ourselves had been different. If we would take this into account we would have
a more critical attitude to ourselves and a more benevolent
one to others.

Remember that among your contemporaries are men of
yesterday, and of today and of tomorrow. All three categories
have immortal souls which must be saved and are worthy
thrice over of every solicitude. But if it is true that there is
more joy in heaven over one sinner who does penance than
over ninety-nine just who think that they need not penance
(and may possibly even to some extent be right about this),
then we also have to say this: if you make a Christian of one
pagan of today who is already actually a man of tomorrow,
then you have done more than by taking care of three of those
who are Christians merely because their parents were. Your
job is not to preserve a folklore-society Christianity but to
win a new world of paganism. Alas, how few there are in the
kingdom of Christ who desire such laurels.

But in all things: strive after love, do not be ashamed of
the gospel, speak the truth of Christ in season and out of season; let your lives always be a clear testimony to your words;
never forget what you are: men with a threefold indelible
seal upon you, men who are the property of God. Speak the
words of sacramental power, bring the bread of life and the
chalice of salvation to a dark and demonic world, proclaim,
in voices now loud, now soft, the message of eternal joy. All
your life long you will have to suffer the apparent experience
of the world's being unchanged by what you do, even though

you pour out into it the last drop of your heart's blood. Have
confidence that your fidelity as priests of Christ will not have
been in vain.

A word to the parents and families of the newly ordained.
You have given a son or brother to the Church. You have
been given in exchange a priest in the family. That is a grace
and blessing for you all. But it is also a task for you. For here
too we must bear one another's burdens. May your sacrifice
of much that is normally bestowed on parents and kin by a
son and brother come down as a blessing upon this priest in
your family. May your prayers go with him. May your
parental or brotherly advice sustain him, as did the words of
Don Bosco's mother to her son. May the undiminished gen-
erosity of the confession of Christ and his Church in spirit
and word and life in your family continue to be, for this
priest who grew up as the fruit of all that richness, a spiritual
home, full of comfort and supporting strength, of which he
can always be thankfully aware as he does his military service
for Christ in the midst of a hostile world. Today a priest is
no longer a man living in unquestioned security in his world
of faith and morals. Like anyone else, he too must renew
each day by prayer the light of faith that is in him and the
power of his heart to will the good. How deeply glad and
thankful he is when others pray with him and bear the burden
with him. Who would have more call to do this than those
whom he now loves not less but more than ever, those who
can today be the first to receive from him a blessing carrying
all the fullness of heaven's blessing and earth's? Truly, such
parents have in the future as much as hitherto the task which
they have been carrying out up to today: to make a daily gift
of their son, through sacrifice, prayer, good advice, and shar-

ing his burdens, to the One to whom he has today been consecrated forever.

And now there is a word to be said to God. But we will speak it where the great thing happened, yesterday and today, which we are joyfully celebrating: at the altar of God, before that body which has today been entrusted to these priests. There we shall utter our inexpressible thanks for the gift which has been given to the ordained in their ordination, and in them to all of us. That is the place for speaking the word in which we invoke God's limitless grace, that he will complete this work, begun today, unto the day of Christ Jesus. That is the place in which to call upon his grace which is without repentance. That is the place, now as on each of the days that are coming, in which to take hold anew on the priestly life as what it is: the presence of the holy common daily life, of happiness in the pains of death, of the word of God in the flesh of this earth. We, the rest of us, are now going with you, your reverences, before the altar, which has become forever the firm central point of your lives, from which every road that you will travel goes out and to which all will return until all your roads have reached their end. We others are going with you to this evening thanksgiving at the end of this day of your first Mass. And you yourselves will, in conclusion, in all the authority and commission of your priesthood, bless us, so that all things may end in blessing.

Appendix

A Basic Ignatian Concept:[1]
Notes on Obedience

In contributing to a periodical which is commemorating the fourth centenary of the death of St. Ignatius, the founder of the Jesuit Order, what theme should a writer choose? If he prefers not to speak of the saint himself directly and still wants a fitting topic, he could choose nothing better than the concept of obedience. Jesuit obedience—some like to call it "cadaver" obedience—is a well-known and even notorious tag. It is also something which is poorly understood. Ignatius stressed the importance of this virtue for members of his Society, since it is a matter of great moment for an order engaged in the active care of souls. But in reality Jesuit obedience does not differ from the obedience found in the other religious orders of the Catholic Church.

In choosing obedience for his topic this writer does not flatter himself that he is rediscovering a long-neglected subject. In the last ten years, in Middle Europe alone, at least fifty books and articles have been devoted to this theme. In attempting to make a few remarks on obedience, the writer is troubled by a suspicion that he may merely want to be numbered among those who have had something to say on the subject. Besides, in a short article like this, one can scarcely hope to say anything that is at all comprehensive or conclu-

sive. Hence these few lines do not pretend to be more than
marginal notes, and the writer is resigned to facing the possible accusation that he was incapable of thinking of a livelier
topic for discussion.

Various Misconceptions

Considered in its essence, obedience in religious life has
nothing to do with the obedience which children owe their
parents and others in authority who are supposedly equipped
to attend to their upbringing. The reason is that this latter
kind of obedience has as its very aim its own eventual transcendence. By means of this training in obedience, the obedience of childhood later becomes superfluous, since the adult,
having achieved liberation from the rule of blind instinctive
drives, is able to command himself. In the case of obedience
in religious life, on the other hand, we assume that the subject is already an adult. But we do not assume that the person
who commands is necessarily more intelligent, more gifted
with foresight, or more mature morally than the person who
obeys. If such an assumption were in order, the relationship
of superior to subject would be an educational one. The person obeying would be a child, or a man of infantile character,
not yet responsible for his own behavior. Human nature being
what it is, there are such persons even in religion. Still, the
percentage of them should not be higher than is found in
other walks of life. And I suppose that, generally speaking,
it is not. After all, childish persons can find too many havens
from their unfitness for life without seeking refuge in religion.

One conclusion that can be drawn from these rather obvious considerations is this: Superiors should not act as if by
nature or by reason of their office they were more intelligent,

cleverer persons, more steadfast morally, more provident and wise in the ways of the world. But it should be soberly stated (for subjects, lest they demand too much of superiors, which would be unjust and uncharitable; for superiors, lest they delude themselves): the higher the office, the slighter the possibility, humanly speaking, that its holder will fill its requirements as well as will a man with a lesser post. For we may reasonably presume that the degrees of variation in mental and moral gifts among men are less than the degrees of difficulty found in the management of various social enterprises. From this it follows unavoidably that, as a rule, more important duties will be more inadequately carried out than lesser ones. No judgment is passed here on any particular case. As a matter of fact, people sometimes do grow in stature in performing more difficult tasks. But for the most part the effects are the opposite. With the assumption of more important responsibility comes the painful realization on the part of both the superior and those around him that the man is far from being equipped for his job. The partial failure in fulfilling heavier obligations cruelly lays bare the shortcomings in a man's capacities which had previously escaped our attention.

Let us repeat once more: obedience in religious life is not the obedience of children. Therefore, the religious superior should not play the role of an Olympian papa. In the life of the cloister (even in orders of women) there are still to be found age-old rituals governing the etiquette of superiors, involving demands for respect from subjects, secretiveness, manifestations of superiority, appeals of superiors to a higher wisdom, displays of condescension, etc. All this should gradually be permitted to wither away. Superiors should cast a long, cool glance at the world around them: people who are really powerful and influential, who receive a great deal of unquestioning obedience, place no value on ceremonial of this sort. They find no need for concealing their weakness, anxiety, and insecurity behind a pompous front. Superiors should quietly admit that in certain circumstances their subjects know more than they do about the matter at hand. Given the specialization of modern life with its need for countless types of ability to cover its many areas, present-day superiors can no longer act as if they had a grasp of any and every matter that comes under their authority. In the good old days a superior could do everything that he commanded his subject to do. He had previously done that very thing himself. He had distinguished himself (otherwise he normally would not have been made superior), and so had given proof that he had at least as much understanding of things as his subject. At least this was the rule in the past, though naturally there were exceptions even then. Today it is quite inevitable that what formerly was the exception should become the rule. Every religious superior has many subjects who necessarily have a knowledge of science, of pastoral functioning, of current affairs, which the superior (who can be a specialist himself only in a single limited field) cannot possess. He finds himself, or ought to find himself, in the same position with regard to the knowledge of others as does a President with respect to the mysteries his atomic experts advise him about.

The superior, therefore, is dependent upon the information of counselors to an extent not required in the past. The advisors, usually provided for superiors by the constitutions of an order, have today in many ways a function that is utterly new, and one of more urgent necessity than in former times when they served in practice only as a democratic check on an excessively authoritarian and uncontrolled government by one individual. It would be well, therefore, if superiors would always seek the information they need in specific detail and in a spirit of objectivity, for they must give commands for objective and concrete situations without regard for any value which might attach to obedience to an objectively erroneous command. This is not always done. A secret-cabinet policy may often be a well-intentioned means of acquiring such objective counsel, but it is not always effective. In religious life, in the final analysis, there can be no real democratization of obedience, as will be shown later. But there can be objective and clearly determined methods of procedure for obtaining the counsel and information needed for decision. Unfortunately they are not always followed. Once again I insist, mostly for the benefit of the secular opponent and hostile critic of religious obedience: the people in religious life realize that religious obedience is not the obedience of children. It does not presuppose children, but mature adults. And only in the measure that it can legitimately make this presupposition can it be at all true to its own proper nature.

Again, religious obedience is no mere "observance of traffic laws." Certainly where men live together in a community there must be order, and if there is to be order, there must be the power to command. Everyone may not do as he pleases; and moreover, not everyone is able to see for himself just what is required by the community as a whole. But a command implies one who obeys. When obedience is conceived merely as a rational, or rationally prescribed, function of order for the life of a community and the co-ordination of its organs and activities towards a common goal, then perhaps a pattern has been discovered which will shed light on civic and national obedience. But in this concept the peculiar nature of religious obedience has not been grasped, even though it cannot be denied that this other aspect of obedience is also present in religious life, and necessarily so. Religious obedience is not a rational and inevitable regulation of traffic by which every sensible person submits himself to the traffic policeman, and in which a co-ordinating agency sees to it that everything moves without friction towards the common good. At times attempts have been made to explain religious obedience in this merely rational fashion. But this explanation is too facile; it cannot reach the real roots and depths of religious obedience. And yet the obedience entailed in the rational regulation of traffic and the sensible co-ordination of work in a common effort is part of religious obedience, though it is not the most characteristic part, nor is it the most profound element of the evangelical counsel. For the daily functioning of obedience in religious life it should be noted that this element of obedience is present: yes, that it is almost identical with the superficial task of quotidian obedience.

For day-to-day life, therefore, a certain demystification of obedience should unobtrusively take place, to a greater extent, perhaps, than is now permitted in some quarters. In the many small details of daily life, obedience is really nothing other than a rational method by which rational beings live together. Therefore the superior should not try to give the impression that he is under the immediate inspiration of the Holy Ghost, but should be courageous enough to seek approval for his orders by giving reasons for them. It is inconceivable that such an approach to mature and much-loved brothers and sisters in the Lord should pose a threat to the authority of the superior, who, according to Christ's command, should see in the authority of his office only the greater obligation to serve. This does not mean that there should be long debates and discussions over every minor decree of a superior. That was the folly of the parliaments in the past. It would be irrational and childish (although unfortunately it does occur). The problem can be met and overcome by an appeal to higher ascetical motives. To avoid exasperating himself or others, the subject should calmly and maturely consider the many inevitable regulations of daily life in a religious community for what they really are: inevitable burdens of earthly life which weigh upon people in the world as heavily as they do on people in the religious life. Much of the friction among religious arising from the details of the common life comes solely from that immaturity which has not grasped the fact that rebelling against communal rules and regulations is not the way for a person to prove his independence and personal integrity. And still it remains true: religious obedience, according to its own proper nature, is more than merely a rational observance of traffic regulations.

There is a third consideration which will preserve religious obedience from misconception and excess. It is not true, even in religious communities, that all initiative should come from superiors. Nor should we be too quick to dismiss this statement as a mere platitude. Really to comprehend it we must make use of metaphysics, a metaphysics which consists in pondering with wonder the commonplace and the obvious and then drawing some conclusions. Human authority (even when exercised in God's name) must not be conceived as adequately and exclusively competent to monopolize all initiative, all effort and all personal decision. Nor does it contain the implication that subjects are called to initiative and decision only when authority gives them the signal.

One frequently gets the impression, both in religious orders and in the Church generally, that initiative, action, militancy, and the like, are indeed considered necessary and desirable in subjects, but only on condition that the go-signal has been given "from above," and only in the direction which has already been unequivocally and authoritatively determined by superiors. Unconsciously and spontaneously a strong tendency is at work to make the subject feel that he is so built in to his order or the Church that only the structure as a whole, through its hierarchy, is capable of initiative; that opinion or enterprise has its legitimacy only in the express, or at least tacit, approval of authority.

Unless we wish to absolutize the community, the principle of subsidiarity must apply not only between smaller and larger societies, but between individuals and their communities as well. Yet there can be none of the subordination of an individual to a community, and to the authority representing it, which tries to make the individual an exclusively dependent function of the community and its authority. We need only put the question in its full simplicity: may one make a request to a superior or, with due modesty, propose an alternative policy? Everyone will answer: "Obviously, yes." Hence it is unnecessary to ask the superior first whether he wants the request to be presented or the alternative proposed. Yet this request, this alternative suggestion, is also an exercise of initiative, in which one must take the responsibility of deciding whether it is to be presented or not. Even when in complete obedience and modesty the decision is left to the superior, the suggestion alters the situation of the superior in making his decision. It broadens or narrows the field of choice. Indeed, even when the subject shows the greatest discretion, the superior is "influenced," whether he likes it or not, whether or not the suggestion involves something he would have done on his own.

There is no autarchic human authority in the whole world which is pure activity, with no element of passivity. To exercise absolute authority is proper only to the Creator, who is not faced with structures in opposition and unavoidable conflicts of initiative, because he himself in the strict sense makes everything out of nothing. Any other authority, even in the Church and in religious orders, is not the one determining initiative, but only one force in an immense network of forces, active and passive, receiving and giving. Authority has the legitimate function of direction, co-ordinating, overseeing, and planning the whole interplay of human initiatives. It is not, strictly speaking, even in the ideal order, so representative of God that it alone is the autarchic planner and designer of all human activity. This would be the hybris of a totalitarian system which could not exist, and, more significantly, should not.

Hence in practice, even in religious orders, authority needs, evokes and employs the initiative of subjects. Even considered in the abstract, there can be no one exercising absolute rule over these human resources. There will always be initiatives arising from sources independent of the authority and beyond its control. Because this is so and cannot be otherwise, it *should* be so. That is to say, in no community or society, not even in the Church or the religious orders, *may* authority act as if it were itself the only source of good initiatives, so that every plan, command, and desire must depend for its origin and execution on this authority alone. Even the most laudable initiatives of the Holy See are only the reactions from actions originating elsewhere, and this is important to note. The same thing holds true for the authorities of religious orders. Subjects are not mere receivers of commands, because that is simply impossible. The aim of obedience is not to make merely passive subjects. This is not even an "asymptotic" ideal, but a chimera; it would be the usurpation of the creative power reserved to God alone, which he can delegate to no one. Only God has "all the threads in his hands," and he has empowered no one to act in his fashion.

Consequently the superior cannot be a god in the exercise of his office. Not to prevent his subjects from assuming initiative is not enough; he must positively count on it, invite it; he must not be irked by it. He must, to a certain degree, recognize himself also as only one of the wheels in a heavenly mechanism whose ultimate and total meaning is decided by one only—God, and no other. The superior always remains himself part of a developmental process. In an ultimate sense, he does not know exactly to what end evolution is moving. In spite of all the authority given him, and in spite of all the supervision he is charged with, he acts in trust and ventures into the unknown. He, too, never clearly knows what effect he is causing or setting in motion when he commands or refrains from commanding. He must remember that his authority is not the only source of the divine impulse, direction, and stimulation. He must realize that God has never taken on the obligation of providing those he has selected and invested with authority with advance information concerning his own activity in the Church for the salvation of souls and the progress of history. The superior has no exclusive vision of the divine will which it is his mission to pass on to his subjects. There is no God-given warrant for such a process of communication. Rather, the superior too must be an obedient man, a hearer. The formal correctness and juridical validity of his commands does not guarantee that they are likewise ontologically sound. If the subject must obey an order so as not to be disobedient in the sight of God, this is not proof that the command given was the one which should have been given according to God's antecedent will. It may be the product of a permitted fault in the superior. It may be derived from lifeless traditionalism, human limitations, routine, a shortsighted system of uniformism, a lack of imagination, and many other factors.

There are a plurality of forces in the world which can in no way be hierarchically subject to authority—though such forces cannot contradict authority in so far as it succeeds in bringing them within the field of direction and command. This latter task, as has been said, can and should be only partially achieved. Hence the subject in religious life has no right simply to shield himself with obedience, as if he could thus be freed from a burden which he himself must bear for the responsible direction of his own personal initiative. We often hear apologias for obedience which praise this supposed advantage of freedom from concern. It does not exist. At least not in the sense that the religious can thereby escape from the burden of personal responsibility. He himself chooses obedience; otherwise he would not be in religious life. He must, then, answer for the consequences of his choice.

The received command is a synthesis of elements. One is the superior's personal and original activity, the other is the external condition for that activity. This condition is constituted by the subject himself, his mode of being and action, his capacities and incapacities (perhaps culpable), his approach to and attitude towards the superior. This conditioning is prior to the command and makes the subject co-responsible for the command itself. Certainly the religious can often say for his own consolation that the superior must answer for this or that decision, and not the subject. But this consolation does not amount to much. The religious cannot escape the responsibility for his own life taken as whole, down to its last details. He simply hears in the command the echo of his own character and activity. There is not in this world any control-center of action from whose uninfluenced motion everything else in existence originates. A human being cannot relinquish his personality to a representative, not even in religious life. That is in no sense the purpose of obedience.

True Obedience

To provide a positive definition of religious obedience is by no means a simple matter. We could immediately and without further ado maintain that religious obedience is an abiding resonance to God's commands and the fulfillment of the divine will. But in that event we should have to determine how it is possible to know the sense in which it can be said that what is commanded is the will of God. For the fact remains that there can be commands the subject must obey —provided the things commanded are not sinful—which in the objective order are wrong, and in given circumstances have been issued with real culpability on the part of the superior. In cases of this kind it is no easy undertaking to say why and in what sense the fulfillment of such an order could be the will of God. Nor should we oversimplify the matter by adverting without qualification to the merits of the "holocaust," the total renunciation of self, which this obedience entails. For it is obvious that pure subjection to the will of another who is not God has in itself no moral value whatsoever. In itself, pure dependence on the will of another is amoral, and may be even immoral, unless there is some further element in the situation.

We might add that if religious obedience is the subordination of one's own will and decisions to those of another who holds the place of God and is the interpreter of the divine will, we must at least be sure of our means of knowing how this other person has received the divine commission to be the expositor of God's will. This question is a difficult one; even more so than that of poverty and of the evangelical counsel to renounce the blessings of conjugal love. For these two evangelical counsels are recommended directly in the words of Holy Scripture and by our Lord himself. As far as these two counsels are concerned, it is always possible to fall back on this recommendation, even when we do not succeed in achieving a crystal-clear understanding of their inner meaning. In this matter it can be said that the religious is walking in the way of the gospels. And to one who has set out on this path in unquestioning surrender the meaning of these counsels will be more and more fully revealed. He can always say that he is imitating Christ. And hence he needs no further argument than that the disciple does not wish to be above his master, and that love comprehends what it recognizes as a fundamental characteristic in the beloved Lord.

Concerning obedience, however, the problem is not as simple as all that. As a matter of fact, we see that in the days

of the early Church, already with its continuous procession
of ascetics and virgins, there was as yet no mention of religious obedience. Nor can any direct affirmation of this concept be found in the pages of the gospels. The early ascetics
lived the life of solitaries, and so there was no stimulus to
evoke an ideal of obedience. And even for a long time after-
wards obedience was not honored as a third vow. The religious
accepted a celibate or monastic life in any form, and obliged
himself to remain in a definite community which lived such a
mode of life. It is clear that we have to proceed carefully if
we are to specify the content and arguments for religious
obedience.

Before we proceed with our inquiry into the precise meaning of obedience as it is practiced in a religious community,
we must be cautioned against another simplification which
would seem to provide a quick and easy solution for those
problems. It will not suffice simply to refer to the example
of Christ. Beyond doubt he was obedient. Obedience to his
Father, as he made plain, was the form, the driving power
and the content of his life. We must by all means imitate
Christ. But the question is precisely this: how do we know that
in the subordination of self to human authority we exercise
the most profound obedience of God? Christ did not do it.
The Apostle is indeed aware of human authorities who in
some fashion take the place of God in our regard and whose
decrees should appear to us to be God's will. But Paul is
speaking of the authorities we have not freely chosen or
created, who existed before us, or before we had any choice
in the matter—namely, parents, masters and civil governors.
Can we extend this dominion of the divine will over us to new
regimes of our own making? If we answer that religious

superiors have ecclesiastical authority, since they are appointed by the Church, this alone does not lead us to any clearcut doctrine. Subordination to the authority of religious superiors is not imposed on men by the Church without their own free and deliberate consent as implied by the vows. Hence the question remains: Why is it meritorious to submit to the authority of another when it has not been imposed on us by God himself? Should we not guard the freedom God has entrusted to us as zealously as our function of personal responsibility, since, as we have said, an absolute surrender of the freedom for which we are innately responsible is in no way possible or reasonable?

Hence the argument for religious obedience from the gospels is not so clear, nor can it be demonstrated immediately or without further examination. Our problem could be summed up in the following question: is religious obedience a concrete prolongation of obedience to the will of God, either in general, as it finds expression in God's commandments, or in particular as it is manifested in God's direction, inspiration and providential disposition of the lives of men?

Religious obedience should certainly not be held to mean obedience to each order that is given, nor is it even the abstract notion of a general readiness to obey every order. Primarily, it is the permanent binding of oneself to a definite mode of life —to life with God within the framework of the Church. It involves the exclusive dedication of one's energies to the concerns of the Lord and to what is pleasing to him. We accept as a form of life the expectation of God's kingdom of grace coming from on high. Obedience is concerned with the sacrifice and renunciation of the world's most precious goods; the renunciation of the right to build a little world of our own as a sphere of freedom through the acquisition of wealth; the renunciation of the right to one's own hearth and the security to be found in the intimate love of another person through the conjugal bond. It is concerned with prayer, and with the testimony to God's grace which is to be found in what is commonly known as the care of souls and the apostolate. Beyond this we need no further description of this life of the evangelical counsels, nor any argument for it.

Obedience is a permanent form of life giving man an orientation toward God. It does so ecclesiologically because by it the religious manifests the specific essence of the Church. It is the manifestation of God's other-worldly grace beyond the reach of earthly merit, to be accepted by faith alone in spite of all human impotence. In this manifestation the Church achieves her existential visibility and becomes historically tangible through doctrine and sacrament. This is the life to which the religious immediately and primarily pledges himself. His obedience with reference to the individual things which a superior may enjoin is specified by this life-form which gives it its definite religious significance. Otherwise there would be no sense to vowed obedience. It would not be a religious matter at all. On the contrary, it would be perverse to attach merit to this kind of obedience in any other field of life; for instance, if one were to vow obedience for the better functioning of a center for chemical research in which one is employed as a collaborator. If we suppose that a permanent vowed obligation to a religious life is of positive value in the moral order (and this is presupposed here), and if we further assume that it is proper and reasonable, though not necessary, to lead such a life in a community, then it follows that obedience to the directors of this community is justified and meaningful in the concrete pursuit of this permanent way of life.

Hence we are not trying to canonize an abstract notion of obedience as the doing of another's will considered in itself. Such abstract obedience is due to God alone, and no transfer to another is permitted. Furthermore, we may not obey purely for the sake of obeying, or of denying our own will. Behavior of this sort, considered abstractly in itself, would not only be without value in the sphere of morality, it would be positively absurd and perverse. The fact that it would be "difficult," a "perfect holocaust," painful and troublesome for one who is obedient at all times and in all things, can scarcely constitute an argument for the meaningfulness of obedience. The implied presupposition of this argument, namely that the more difficult and repugnant thing is always the better and the more pleasing to God, just because it means a renunciation painful for man, cannot be the legitimate starting-point of discussion.

Our concept of obedience also explains why religious obedience has its place exclusively in a religious society approved and sanctioned by the Church. The content of obedience must be guaranteed if this obedience is to possess moral value. It is not enough that commands shall be morally indifferent. They must be morally good in their total context. The totality must represent the content of the evangelical counsels to the world on behalf of the Church. One can make a vow only in reference to a higher good. Thus one may not vow directly, and as an end in itself, to do something which under certain circumstances becomes—even if not sinful—less prudent, less good, less meaningful. It follows from this in the first place that the proper and essential object of re-

ligious obedience is a permanent way of life in accordance
with the evangelical counsels, for the certain teaching of the
Church is that this is the higher good. However, the nature
of this superiority will not be further explained here.

Obedience is definitely not to be conceived as the "heroic"
(foolhardy, almost) granting of *carte blanche* to a superior,
with the result that the religious simply does not do his own
will, either because of the constant pleasure he would take
in it—which makes its renunciation difficult—or because this
course is fraught with danger, and hence is to be avoided. For
this reason obedience is always specified with reference to the
constitutions of a given order, and the superior may only
command within the framework set by the constitutions. In
seeking the real essence of obedience, the most important
point is missed if only the particular command of the superior
is primarily and abstractly considered according to the formula:
I declare myself ready to execute the command of another
if this command is not evidently immoral. This is not what is
meant. Obedience is the acceptance of a common mode of
religious life in imitation of Christ according to a constitu-
tion which the Church has acknowledged to be a true and
practical expression of a divinely oriented existence. By virtue
of this acceptance and obligation the vow explicitly or im-
plicitly includes the carrying out of the just commands of
the authority, necessary in any society, when they are directed
to the concrete realization of the life-form of religious com-
mitment "according to the constitutions." Such concrete
instances cannot be determined *a priori* once and for all. Therefore, one who is critical of the idea of religious obedience is
really attacking the wisdom of the life of the counsels in the
Church. Moreover, he is attacking the wisdom of a life that

is not primarily concerned with the tangible realization of worldly objectives, but which through faith makes the expectation of hidden grace the ground of existence, and translates this faith into act. Without such an act, faith itself would be meaningless. This act is representative of the Church and bears the Church's witness to the world. If this mode of existence is to have meaning, then, it must inspire a willingness to carry out in any given instance the concrete actions, undertakings and renunciations held to be necessary for its concrete realization in the judgment of competent authority.

This is why obedience is connected with the teaching and example of Christ, who was obedient even to the death of the cross. Whoever enters into a religious community, whoever perpetually and irrevocably makes this way of life his own, chooses for himself an unforeseeable destiny. For the consequences of such an election and dedication to the community and its rationale of action cannot be foreseen in detail. All these consequences can be difficult and painful. But this gamble (considered in its formal structure) is involved in every human obligation whereby another person with his own proper will becomes an inseparable part of one's own life. We find it in marriage, in the acceptance of the duties of citizenship, in the responsibility of office, and so forth. Hence, if the religious community and its basic ideals are justified and meaningful (which in our case we legitimately assume to be true), so too is the obligation toward all its consequences which cannot be seen in advance. A human mode of life which consists in the free subordination to something higher than itself cannot exist without this element of risk. And without such a surrender the individual will remain in his own egotism behind the defenses of his own existential anxiety,

which is the surest way to destruction. But the man who gives
himself to what is higher and nobler, who takes the gamble,
knows that he is only doing what Christ himself did in his
obedience.

Under this aspect, that which in a given instant is irrational and indefensible, but is genuinely unavoidable, really
becomes the will of the Father. In this way the crucifixion of
Christ, a crime of Jews and pagans, "had" to be; it was the
will of the Father who had planned it, even though it came
about only as the result of the shortsightedness and guilt of
men. The permanent dedication to the ideal of the counsels in
imitation of Christ, who was poor and self-denying, the crucified legate of God consecrated to prayer and atonement, is
lived all but exclusively in a community professing the same
ideal. Hence the obedience it entails must be regarded as the
will of God, even if a particular command appears to be
senseless (just as death, failure and the other tragic circumstances of human life appear to be), provided, of course, that
what is commanded is not immoral in itself. Religious obedience is thus a participation in the cross of Christ.

Nor should one protest that the irrationality of a mistaken
command frees the subject from his contract, and obedience
to it cannot be considered as a share in Christ's mission. We
must realize that religious obedience is more than a rationally
accepted agreement governing "traffic arrangements" in a common enterprise, though this is, of course, included, since life in
any community demands such obedience. In our case community life is directed to God. In any other society, obedience
to an unwise command could be justified only by the reflection that such unavoidable eventualities must be accounted
part of the original bargain. Otherwise obedience, which is

always necessary to some degree, would end, for it would always be left to the discretion of the subject to obey. But in religion the imitation of Christ is practiced. There the cross of Christ is considered not merely as something inevitable, or as the pain of life, by and large to be evaded, but rather as the embodiment of grace and its acceptance through faith, as something which "must" be, "so that the Scriptures might be fulfilled," since only "thus" can one enter into one's glory. There the command which is judged unwise according to its immediate historical context will be seen as something which in the framework of religious life is of value, and even desirable. This does not, of course, justify the superior in issuing it. Yet such an order can have the same meaning as the one the saints, in their imitation of Christ, found in failure, shame, the shattering of cherished plans, martyrdom, and every other variety of undeserved suffering. They secretly longed for these things as the embodiment of their faith in God's grace now reaching its perfection.

It might be in place here to recognize that a personal morality and spontaneous moral judgment have a greater function in religious obedience than is commonly supposed. The command of a superior may be objectively sinful, and if recognized as such by the inferior it should not be put into execution. Everyone will agree that a superior, even with the best intentions, can issue an order which is objectively wrong. If one does not consider as sins only those things which are expressly labeled as such in confessional manuals, then it will be hard to deny that what is materially false can also very often be objectively immoral. What is more, it is not easy to explain why this is not generally so. Let us invent an example. A higher superior tells the principal of a boarding school that he must under all circumstances make the boys go to confession once a week. Suppose that the subordinate, in this case the principal of the boarding school, clearly realizes what the superior in his idealistic remoteness from life cannot comprehend—namely, that such a demand will eventually prove very harmful to the spiritual life of his charges. Question: have we here merely a case of ill-conceived pedagogical instructions which must be carried out because this is an order, or have we in fact a demand which, however innocently made, is unjustified; an order which, since it actually poses a serious threat to the genuine spiritual development of these youths, should not be carried out by the subordinate? The imprudence of the practice of itself offends moral principles. Must the subject now declare that he cannot square it with his conscience and ask to be relieved of his office? Reading the older moralists, one gets the impression that they were more concerned with such cases than we are today. Have we today become more moral, or has the principle "an order is an order" gained a foothold even in such holy places as religious communities? Do we avoid talking about such possibilities for fear of the harm done by the conscientious objector, and so act as if something of this kind practically never occurred? But is not the consequent harm done to consciences a matter of graver importance than the utility of smoothly functioning external government, requiring of subjects a literal obedience to commands? Even the subject has the duty in conscience of examining the moral admissibility of what has been commanded. The just "presumption" that the command of a superior will be morally unobjectionable not only subjectively but also objectively does not constitute a simple dispensation from the essential obligation of every man to attain moral certitude as to whether a free action is morally licit before it is undertaken. The simple fact that it is commanded makes this action no less his own and no less one for which he will be responsible.

As a religious grows older he asks himself with a deep, secret anxiety whether he has done anything in his life which can endure judgment in God's sight. Nothing, of course, can so endure, except what he has given out of pure mercy. What is worthy of God comes from God's grace alone. It is for this very reason that it matters what one does. There is a total difference between man's potentialities when God's grace is accepted and when it is rejected. God has told us—and he is greater than the human heart—that there are such things as acts of selfless devotion, obedience to God's holy will and self-forgetting dedication. Yet we are constantly discovering in ourselves—those of us who are not stupid, naive or conceited—things which fill us with the fear that there is nothing in us but egotism—both patent and disguised. Do we know for certain that God's grace has ever been operative in us? Such an event should have transformed our lives. Yet has there ever been a moment when we have not been seeking ourselves, when our success has not been the fruit of egotism, when our love for God has not been a form of anxiety, when what we thought of as patient prudence was not really faint-heartedness? The divine work of healing is accomplished in divers marvelous ways, giving us the right to hope that not everything in our life has been open or covert self-seeking. Nor need our painful anxiety about our state be interpreted as another manifestation of self-seeking or a veiled attempt at self-justification before God.

Anyone who experiences this kind of anxiety has reduced

his life to an easy and essential simplicity. We are on our own, but the last and most important action will be accomplished in us by God himself, working through the bitterness of life itself. This individual can always do one thing at least, he can yield himself up to something greater than himself. He can also see to it that this greater Reality shall be more than an ideal or a theory which, in the final analysis, is under his own control and can be altered according to his whim, so that it is no longer distinguishable from the mere idols of the heart. The individual can strive to make this nobler Reality actual in his life. This Reality must make demands on us when we do not want to be constrained; must exert its effects even when we do not want it to; must cause us suffering we ourselves would rather avoid. This happens when the greater Reality to which we dedicate ourselves becomes a tangible force of incomprehensible power whose word of command is addressed to us—and we obey.

This means to obey silently, and in the true sense unquestioningly; to serve, and to submit to a demand we have not ourselves invented. When this happens we have too little time and too little interest to defend or develop our personal integrity. The self has lost its importance. We might even be so fortunate as to become a true person who comes alive in so far as he forgets and sacrifices himself, in so far as he obeys. But we must remember that the good fortune of life is God's grace. In order to become obedient, and in transcendence lose ourselves—the only way of ever really finding ourselves—we must perhaps see nothing at all extraordinary in obedience, hardly ever think of it reflexively. We should rather think of the Reality we serve as a matter of course. That Being is worthy of all love and service, because ultimately it is no mere cause but *the Person:* God. Perhaps the truly obedient man is simply the lover, for whom the sacrifice of self-surrender is sweet, a blessed delight. Perhaps we should not talk so much about obedience, for it is already threatened when we praise or defend it. Either tactic is only meaningful as an encouragement for the young, in order to strengthen their wills to embrace in silence a matter-of-course service of God in the Church through a life of prayer and witness. They must learn that this is meaningful even though the heart shudders and the wisdom of this world is in panic at the thought of losing self in the loss of freedom. The ultimate obedience, that which demands and silently takes everything, will be exacted by God alone. It is the command to die the death which overshadows every minute of our life, and detaches us from ourselves more and more. This command, to move on and to leave all, to allow ourselves in faith to be absorbed in the great silence of God, no longer to resist the all-embracing, nameless destiny which rules over us—this command comes to all men. The question whether man obediently accepts it is decisive for time and eternity. The whole of religious life grounded in obedience is nothing more than a rehearsal, a practical anticipation of this situation, which envelops human existence more and more. For the religious it is the participation in the death of Christ and the life concealed in him.

Note

[1] The German original of this article: "Eine ignatianische Grunghaltung," appeared in *Stimmen der Zeit*, 158 (1955-6), pp. 253-267. The present translation was made collectively under the direction of Joseph P. Vetz, S.J., and the supervision of Gustave Weigel, S.J.

Notes on Sources

Serving Human Beings

"Paul, Apostle for Today," paper read July 24, 1958, to the Paulus-Gesellschaft, Frankfurt am Main.

"Railway Missions," paper read April 25, 1955, to conference of societies for the protection of young girls, published in *Aus unserer Arbeit*, 3, Freiburg (1955), pp. 1-13.

"Parish and Place of Work," paper read to conference of Betriebsmännerwerke in Düsseldorf, 1953, published as *Seelsorge und Betrieb*, Cologne (1953); translated into Dutch in *Binnenlands apostolaat*, 5 (1954), pp. 83-104; published in *Stimmen der Zeit*, 153 (1954), pp. 401-12, and in *Anima*, 10 (1955), pp. 180-88.

"The Prison Pastorate," paper read June 23, 1959, to conference of prison chaplains in Innsbruck, published in *Der Seelsorger*, 29 (1959), pp. 460-69.

"Theology of Books," paper read March 16, 1959, to conference of the book apostolate in Cologne, published in *Kölner Pastoralblatt*, 11 (1959), pp. 144-8, 205-11, 229-31.

Spirituality for the Pastor

"The Theological Meaning of Devotion to the Heart of Jesus," given at Canisius College, Innsbruck, June 12, 1953, published in the college newsletter, no. 88 (1953), pp. 1-10.

"Ignatian Spirituality and Devotion to the Heart of Jesus," given at Canisius College, Innsbruck, June 1955, published in the college newsletter, no. 90 (1955-56), pp. 5-17, translated into French in *Les Carnets du Sacré Coeur*, 13 (1956), pp. 25-43, and *Revue d'Ascetique et de Mystique*, 35 (1959), pp. 147-66.

"First Mass," given at the German College, Rome, October 11, 1955, published in *Salzburger Klerusblatt*, 88 (1955), pp. 221 f. and in the college newsletter, no. 63 (1956), pp. 26-31.

"Notes on Obedience," *Stimmen der Zeit*, 158 (1956), pp. 253-67, translated into English in *Woodstock Letters*, 86, no. 4 (1957), pp. 291-310.